THE BRITISH LIBRARY GUIDE TO

Writing and Scripts

Multi-lingual/multi-scriptual Coca Cola logo.

This gives some idea of the range of major writing systems and scripts in use today.
Throughout the history of writing there have been hundreds upon hundreds.
These languages are, from left to right, English, Thai, Arabic, Russian (Cyrillic Style),
Amheric, Japanese, Chinese, Hebrew, Korean, and English.

THE BRITISH LIBRARY GUIDE TO

Writing and Scripts

HISTORY AND TECHNIQUES

Michelle P. Brown

UNIVERSITY OF TORONTO PRESS

Front cover illustrations:
Background: Characters from an inscribed Chinese
bronze vessel from the Western Zhou period;
1050–771BC. British Museum Department of
Oriental Antiquities; 1930-11-8-2 (11).
Inset: A scribe in his study. Valerius Ma imus,
'Faits et dits mémorables'. Bruges, 1479.
British Library, MSS, Royal 18 E iii, f.24

First published 1998 by
The British Library
96 Euston Road
London NW1 2DB

Published in North and South America in 1998 by
University of Toronto Press Incorporated
Toronto and Buffalo

Canadian Cataloguing in Publication Data

Brown, Michelle P.
        The British Library Guide to Writing and
Scripts: history and techniques

(The British Library Guides)
Includes bibliographical references and index.
ISBN 0-8020-8172-X

1. Writing - History. 2. Paleography. I. Title. II.
Series.

Z105.B76 1998   417.7
C98-930807-3

Designed and typeset by Andrew Shoolbred
Colour origination by Culver Graphics
Printed in Italy by Grafiche Milani, Milan

Contents

Acknowledgements

I should like to thank the following for their continued support and encouragement, and for their input to this project: my colleagues at the British Library, especially Janet Benoy, Karen Brookfield, Yu-Ying Brown, Brett Dolman, Kathleen Houghton, Geraldine Kenny, Jerry Losty, Beth McKillop, Ann Payne, Laurence Pordes, Andrew Prescott, Alan Sterenberg, David Way, Frances Wood, Anne Young; Michael Clanchy, Albertine Gaur, Uta Frith and other fellow members of the Literacy Seminar of the Cognitive Development Unit of the Medical Research Council; Richard Parkinson and the incomparable Irving Finkel of the British Museum; Phil Healey, Patricia Lovett, Philip Poole, Satwinder Sehmi and Sally Teague; and, as ever, my husband, Cecil Brown. I should like to dedicate this work to a dear friend, Linda Brownrigg, who has provided much valued personal support over the years and whose selfless efforts to provide an interdisciplinary meeting ground for those interested in medieval manuscripts ('the Seminar in the History of the Book to 1500') have made such a significant contribution to manuscript studies internationally.

ONE

Why writing?

Systems of information transmission and the relationship between thought, sound, word and image

Writing is about communication. In our own multi-media age we are well aware that writing is only one part of this process, that it co-exists with a developed oral culture of telecommunications, film and recorded sound, and that, through our television and computer screens and our popular press, it enjoys a complex inter-relationship with sound and image. Nonetheless, writing is as important as ever and still occupies an almost talismanic position in our societies. Knowledge is power; writing remains the principal conveyor of information, and access to writing unlocks the secrets of human knowledge and identity. This was the line of thought that guided Ptolemy Philadelphus, the founder of the first great world library at Alexandria in the third century BC. The 500,000 or so scrolls to be gathered, copied and held there would embody the societies of the day and their cultures and would give Ptolemy the key to their conquest and successful governance. Our modern libraries seek to extend such facilities to all people, giving them the power, intellectually, to govern their own lives.

The human perception of the need to transmit a body of knowledge or information across time and space has been the secret of writing's success. Our memory as individuals forms a large part of who we are. Likewise, group memory is the key to cultural identity. But is writing the only option for preserving and transmitting memory?

Oral tradition

Oral tradition and writing have an overlap. Certain types of information are better suited to being committed to memory than others. Literary information is generally more easily retained (with the assistance of mnemonic devices such as enumeration and alliteration) than extensive numeric data, for example. The limited capacity of human memory is an important factor and has an impact upon the type of information generated by a society. The retention of a large body of exciting information, such as epic tales or poems, for oral recitation may hinder an analytical approach to this information and also the development of new knowledge. Within oral cultures the human memory is primarily allocated to storing information, leaving little room to manipulate it constructively, or to carry on adding to it or developing it. As when a computer's memory is full, the system goes into overload.

Conversely, reliance upon writing, or whatever form of graphic communication, to store information, tends to weaken the power of memory. We become lazy and may relinquish the burden of processing information and carrying as much in our brains as we might. Such can be the case with the compulsion to capture an experience: as with a photograph, which can hinder us from fully savouring and absorbing the event at the time – we know we have captured it and it is there for us to pick out and consume at our leisure – writing can help us to remember, but it can also become the memory itself, a frozen two-dimensional thing. The ability to photocopy written material can also increase this tendency to capture information rather than assimilate it.

The strength and discipline of oral tradition has its own advantages. These are often bolstered by elitism and religious taboos. A sophisticated example of an oral society was that of the Iron Age Celts (fig. 1) who, from around 600 BC onwards, began to spread throughout much of Europe and even into parts of Greece and Asia Minor until confined by the might of Rome and its 'barbarian' successors to the western and northern parts of Britain, and to Ireland and Brittany. Their long-lived hegemony resided largely in their common linguistic and cultural tradition, rather than in any sustained political alliance. This tradition was the preserve of the *Aes Dana*, the privileged learned and artisan classes, which included the druids, an elite body of highly trained preservers of group knowledge in their capacity as shamans, bards and

1. The Dying Gaul, Syon House.

A romanticised Roman image of the Celts, whose culture was based upon sophisticated oral tradition.

2. The Táin Bó Cuailnge. BL, MSS, Egerton MS 93, ff. 29v–30.

A 16th-century Irish copy of an epic tale 'The Cattle Raid of Cooley' which may first have been composed for oral recitation during the Iron Age.

jurists. A rigorous training period of up to 20 years (7–12 years to become a professional bard, a member of the *fili*) was required in special druidic schools before qualifying as a guardian and oral transmitter of such knowledge. Classical sources indicate that the druids were well acquainted with written Greek and Latin, which probably inspired the form of a limited Celtic script called ogham (after the Celtic god of eloquence, literature and the sun, Ogmios/Ogma), but that they eschewed the use of writing in favour of a purer, more rigorous oral tradition, which also safeguarded their elitist status and power. This situation also prevailed in early Indian society, where the Vedas and the Buddhist canon were originally preserved by memory rather than the 'less reliable' written form.

An appreciation of the talismanic power of writing amongst the early Celts is, however, apparent in a passage from the Táin Bó Cuailnge ('The Cattle Raid of Cooley'; fig. 2), an epic tale involving the hero Cú Chulainn which is thought to have been composed during the Iron Age and transmitted orally until committed to writing during the early Christian period. Here a great army is stopped in its tracks by an ogham inscription carved on a stick. Ogham inscriptions (fig. 3) are found on stone in Ireland and parts of the western seaboard of Britain

3. A Celtic ogham inscription with Latin translation, commemorating Maglocunus son of Clutorius; 5th–6th cent. AD, reused as a window sill in Nevern Church, Pembs., Wales.

4. The Celtic ogham alphabet (Satwinder Sehmi, after A. ROSS).

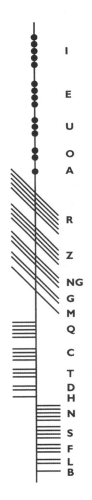

under Irish influence from the 4th to 6th centuries AD but, consisting as they do of characters which are essentially exploded linear forms of Latin letterforms arranged around a base-line, they are only suitable for short commemorative inscriptions. The occurrence of ogham on these stones has led archaeologists to suggest that the script was not invented until that period of heightened contact with the late Roman empire and the post-Roman Church, but an older Iron Age origin is suggested by several references to ogham in the early epic cycles (unless such references represent the intrusion of Christian scribes when committing these tales to writing at a later date).

Not until the widespread conversion of the Celts to Christianity from the 5th century onwards was full 'literacy' achieved, allowing them to act as heirs to what remained of the literate tradition of late Antiquity and the early Christian world. Their long background of oral learning enabled them to make distinctive contributions to this written tradition, leading to the development of one of the most precocious written vernaculars in the West and to the enhancement of the Word of God with the artwork which had for centuries been synonymous with authority and achievement. This often deeply symbolic ornament was now applied to that new symbol of power – the book – enabling the creation of the great Insular gospel books such as the Lindisfarne Gospels (see fig. 63) and the Book of Kells, where the word itself becomes a sacred icon. A sophisticated oral society could bring a unique contribution and enhanced perception to the uses of writing.

The introduction of writing does not necessitate the loss of oral transmission. They can exist in tandem. To pursue the Celtic example, committing tales such as the Táin to writing did not end their oral life.

The bardic tradition continued and from about 1910–30 a curator of manuscripts at the British Museum Library, Robin Flower, spent time on the Blasket Islands off of the west coast of Ireland recording the oral tradition of the area, notably as preserved by Peig Sayers, one of the last of the great Celtic bards, many of whose tales lay in direct descent from their Iron Age prototypes, stretching back over 2,000 years of disciplined oral tradition.

Mnemonic and other simple forms of graphic message transmission

Some of the most basic forms of non-oral message transmission are simple devices to assist memory recall. Amongst these are permanent mnemonic forms such as Australian churingas (semi-abstract carvings on wood or stone depicting totemic creatures which might denote clan origins and ancestors during 'dream time'), knotted cords such as ancient Peruvian quipus which, like knotted handkerchiefs, enjoy a universal currency as *aides-mémoires*, genealogy staffs from New Zealand (fig. 5), Celtic and Australian message sticks and moche marked message beans which were carried by runners around pre-Incan Peru. Other devices such as native American wampum belts (fig. 6) and Nigerian cowrie shells transmit simple messages by the use of numbers or colour. In such a way a Yoruban suitor in Nigeria might signal his attraction by sending his beloved six cowrie shells, *efa* meaning both 'six' and 'attracted' – evidently an effective 'chat-up line' and a simple version of the rebus, which we shall encounter shortly. The Iroquois of northern America might signal their displeasure with their neighbours by sending a wampum belt woven in black (colour denoting mood) and carrying a depiction of a tomahawk in red. The recipient would surely get the message.

Some of the earliest types of information to be recorded in a permanent graphic form relate to property in the form of tallies and property marks. Perhaps the earliest of these, encountered from 4,000 BC

5. Genealogy staff of the Ngati-rangi-toke tribe, from New Zealand. BM, Ethno., 54–12–29.22.

6. Iroquois wampum belt, from N. America. BM, Ethno., 1906.5–23–1.

11

7. Property mark on a seal from Mohenjodaro, the Indus Valley, *c.* 2500–2000 BC. BM, Or., 1947–4–16–1.

onwards, were the early Mesopotamian *calculi* (small clay objects bearing marks indicating amounts) and *bullae* (clay envelopes shaped like balls containing tokens and numerically marked on the outside, like modern bank deposit envelopes). These were not actually writing. More pertinent are the pictographic tablets carrying pictures and numeric marks for goods, along with an imprint of the owner's personal mark or seal, which are known from the region between the Tigris and the Euphrates from around 3,200 BC. Likewise the property marks of the Indus Valley (Pakistan), dating from around 2,300 BC, carry animal or other signs (some 300 of which have been identified) along with writing which remains undeciphered (fig. 7). Most societies have used tallies at some point, whether they be notched door posts, the strung rods (kupe) of the Torres Strait Islands (fig. 8), the Incan administrative knotted cord (quipu) or the wooden tally sticks introduced into the English bureaucracy around 1100 and which continued in use until 1834 when their disposal caused the conflagration which destroyed much of the Palace of Westminster and led to the construction of the existing Houses of Parliament.

Pictography (picture writing) and literal graphic representation

The easiest way of conveying thought and messages is through pictures which transcend linguistic boundaries. Such pictures have been used since at least the time of the earliest prehistoric cave paintings. Native American 'winter count' skins are literal visual representations on hides of the tribe and an annalistic (yearly) record of events, depicted by distinctive images of warfare, plague and the like (fig. 9). Modern signs for roads, toilets, and 'no smoking' areas form a univer-

8. Kupe (tally) from the Torres Strait Islands. BM, Ethno., 89 + 122.

OPPOSITE:
9. Native American winter count skin of the Dakota. BM, Ethno., 1942.AM.7–2.

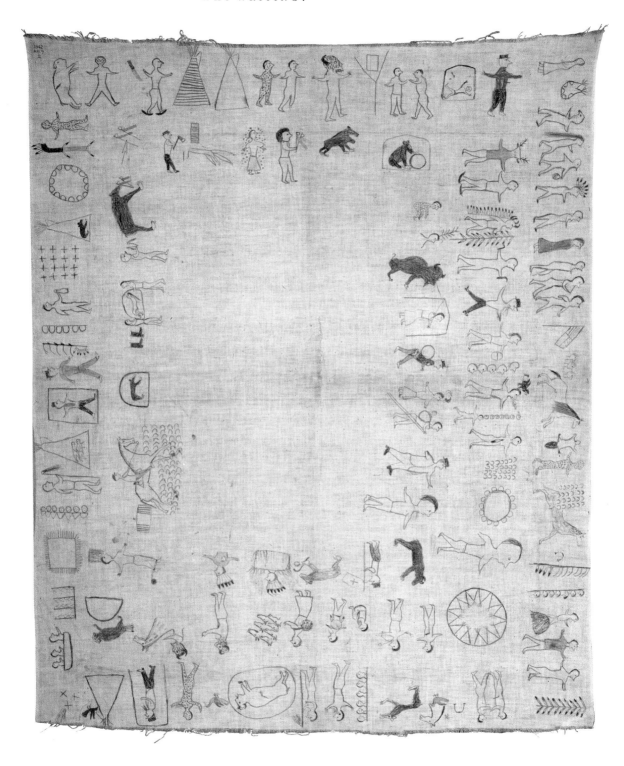

sal language of their own and personal computers increasingly use graphical interfaces, such as icons. Other pictograms assume a level of cognitive association on the part of the audience. The images on posters and advertisements can often only be understood if you are already 'in the know'. Likewise, Kurdish rugs, Welsh love spoons and Aran sweaters carry all sorts of meaning in their abstract decoration, but you need to have been told how to interpret them.

Pictography (picture writing) can, in its most developed form, become iconography, in which the images have recognised cultural connotations which relate to a complex underlying literature. Religious iconography is a good example of this: for example in western illuminated manuscripts, where an image of a woman carrying a palm (symbol of martyrdom) and accompanied by a wheel is automatically read as a depiction of St Catherine who was martyred on a wheel, or a stag is known from Christian exegesis (commentary) to symbolise Christ and a dragon the devil.

We are only now beginning to rival the people of the Middle Ages in their exploitation of the subtle symbiosis which can exist between word and image. However, advanced systems of image-based communication require an underlying system of reference, as does writing. Even the simplest pictorial symbols may require a knowledge of context. For example, a sign consisting of a bottle with a red bar across it might mean 'no alcohol/no drinking' at the entrance to a football stadium, whereas on a train window it would more naturally signify 'do

10. The iconography of the 'horned Moses', The Henry of Blois Psalter, Winchester, *c.* 1150. BL, MSS, Cotton Nero C.iv, f. 4 (detail).

An example of needing to know how to read an image, and that in this case the horns denote Moses, not the Devil.

not throw bottles out of the window', although 'do not drink on the train' is also possible. The inherent ambiguity is a weakness of pictography. A more complex iconographic example from medieval Christian art is that of a horned man. This could theoretically represent either the Devil/a demon or the 'horned Moses', the latter image perhaps deriving from a misunderstanding of a passage of the Old Testament in which Moses is described as 'radiant', mistranslated by the Anglo-Saxons as 'horned' (fig. 10). The viewer needs to know how to read the image in context. In a similar fashion we require a system of reference and context when reading text. To take an example using punctuation: we might be inclined to read 'Stop! Stop!! Stop!!!' as rising in volume to a shout, unless we remember that exclamation marks can also convey emphasis or a sense of urgency, or we go on to read '"Stop! Stop!! Stop!!!" she whispered'.

Pictograms can sometimes become extremely stylised and develop into a form of writing, no longer recognisable simply as images. Such was the case with Mesopotamian cuneiform script (*see* fig. 17) in which a stylus, usually of reed, was used to form impressions on clay and, in so doing, converted simple linear and curved pictograms to stylised symbols formed of individual wedges (hence cuneiform, from Latin *cuneus* – wedge, *forma* – form). Only the earliest clay tablets of the Sumerians of southern Mesopotamia, dating from around 3,300 BC and found at Uruk, were purely pictographic, however. Cuneiform script is more properly a mixed system, as discussed below.

11. Use of the rebus in a children's book, from Catherine Sinclair, *The First...* (1864). BL, 012804.h.13.

Logography, the rebus and the development of ideography (thought writing)

An extension of pictography is logography, in which a symbol denotes a word or words, often in pictographic form, such as the sign on a gentlemen's WC denoting the words 'man/men', or 'gents' washroom'. The early advent of signs denoting numerals may also be relevant in this

15

context. However, the number of pictograms or logograms which would be needed to encompass all ideas would be immense and very limited in nuances. Consequent upon the development of pictography was the idea of using a pictogram not to depict the object itself, but something with a similar sound – the rebus ('the enigmatic representation of name, word etc. by pictures etc. suggesting its syllables'). This assumes a knowledge of language on the part of the reader. To give an example from Victorian children's books, a letter would be written partly using words and partly images of the rebus variety; thus the 'dear' of 'dear Aunt' would be depicted by a deer (fig. 11). We are back to the inarticulate lovelorn Nigerian youth and his six cowrie shells again.

In addition to pictograms and the rebus there is ideography, in which graphic symbols represent ideas, or logography, in which they represent words. An interesting example of this is the Moso script of the Naxi people of south-west China, whose language belongs to the Yi Branch of Tibeto-Burman languages (fig. 12). This is almost completely ideographic/logographic with pictographic symbols being written for essential words, and supplemented by only a small number of supporting phonetic syllabic signs. However, only a limited amount of information can be conveyed by this restricted set of signs and an interpreter is necessary in the person of the hereditary Naxi priests who are trained to memorise and interpret the symbols. The Moso pictographs are thought to have evolved around the thirteenth century AD and continue in use. They provide us with a link back to the origins of Egyptian hieroglyphs and Chinese characters through their pictographic form and religious use.

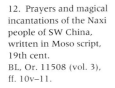

12. Prayers and magical incantations of the Naxi people of SW China, written in Moso script, 19th cent.
BL, Or. 11508 (vol. 3), ff. 10v–11.

Much of the world's population still uses an ideographic (some prefer to see it as logographic) form of writing which originated nearly 4,000 years ago – Chinese script and its derivatives. The Chinese

13. Chinese oracle bone, c. 1600 BC.
BL, Or. 7694/1554.

Such bones were used in divination and carry the earliest Chinese writing.

system worked from a pictographic base, using stylised drawings of things in combination with one another to convey ideas. This resulted in a tremendous number of characters and composite characters. Though phonetic loans helped to create many of these characters in the distant past, for example borrowing the rarely-used ideograph for an unusual grass (pronounced *lai*) to represent the verb 'to arrive, to come' (also pronounced '*lai*'), the script is not tied to the spoken language. All literate people throughout China (and, in the past, Japan, Korea and Vietnam, too) use and understand the Chinese script though they might not understand each others' speech. Thus speakers of the southern Cantonese dialect or coastal Fujianese who might not find the speech of a northern Chinese easy to understand, all use the same script, with a very few, standard, variations.

Most of the earliest extant Chinese characters (about 4,500 of them) occur on oracle bones used for royal divination in the later Shang dynasty around 1,400–1,200 BC (figs 13–14). Some, but by no means all, of the Shang signs are obviously pictographic in origin and are the ancestors of modern Chinese characters such as those for 'tree', 'door' and 'field'. During the Zhou dynasty (*c.* 1,028–221 BC) the range and style of characters was expanded by local modifications, reflecting political and cultural disunity. Unification under the Qin (221–206 BC)

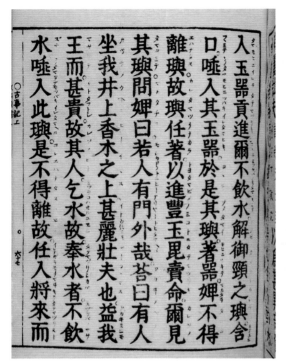

14a. Chinese characters in square style, with accompanying *katakana* to indicate the Japanese reading of a Chinese text. From *Kojiki* ('Ancient Writing of Japan'). Woodblock printed, 1803.
BL, 010C 16047.b.10.

OPPOSITE:
14b. Diagram of Chinese characters, some reflecting an ultimately pictographic origin. (Artwork John Cayley)

occasioned standardisation of the script. By the end of the Han dynasty (206 BC–AD 220), a regular form of the script had emerged, *kai shu*, which is still in use today. Cursive styles developed from the *kai shu* as *shu fa*, 'the art of writing', was elevated to the highest art form in China.

Chinese characters have been classified by groups: pictograms; representational characters (for example conveying the words 'one', 'two' etc. by a corresponding number of horizontal lines); compound representational, which convey ideas by combining characters (for example sun and moon together = 'bright'); the rebus, in which a character can also represent something that sounds the same; and semantic-phonetic, in which characters indicating the meaning of the word and its pronunciation are combined. An imperially commissioned dictionary of 1716 which included all the obscure variant characters known, reached a total of almost 49,000.

When classifying characters for dictionary use, the favoured system is by one of 214 'radicals' or meaning elements plus the residual number of strokes. Phonetic syllabaries, such as that compiled by the missionary W. E. Soothill in the 1880s, were geared to western users at first and, because they required knowledge of a standard rather than of dialect pronunciation, were not used by many Chinese. Since the 1920s, however, alphabetical order has been combined with the traditional dictionary arrangement.

From 1919 a major aspect of Chinese nationalism was a project to reverse the functional illiteracy of the mass of the population through language reform. Pursuing this to achieve what De Francis has termed 'mass literacy through the simplification of characters', the Communist government of China introduced in 1955 a number of simplified characters, many based on ancient cursive forms, involving far fewer strokes than the standard characters. In 1958, *pinyin* ('spell sound'), a locally-produced system of romanisation to transcribe characters, was introduced, partly to help language teaching and partly to counter for-

18

	Oracle Bone Script *Jiaguwen* or Great Seal *Dazhuan**	Small Seal (regularized) *Xiaozhuan*	Traditional Regular Script *Zhenshu* (handwritten style *kaiti*)	Simplified Script *Jiantizi* (printed typeface *songti*)
mu 'wood' (pictographic)			木	木
men 'door' (pictographic)			門	门
tian 'field' (pictographic)			田	田
er 'two' (ideographic)			二	二
ming 'bright' (ideographic compound)			明	明
yun 'to say' ('rebus' borrowing: pictograph 'cloud' used for similar-sounding 'to say')			云	云
jie 'boundary' (semantic-phonetic: 'field' for sense; other element for sound)			界	界
shu 'writing' (pictographic)			書	书
fa 'rules' (semantic-phonetic: with additional elements) *shufa* = 'calligraphy'			法	法

19

eign transcription systems. School children who already knew how to speak their language were taught *pinyin* and then taught characters grouped by pronunciation. Those who did not speak the standard dialect (known in the West as Mandarin) first had to learn that. Thus people of the Chinese linguistic group have to learn and remember a large vocabulary of words/concepts along with their corresponding graphic symbol. The high rate of literacy in East Asia indicates that this feat is not beyond the capacity of the human brain, and anyway, a European language also involves memorising the alphabet and a large vocabulary of words, grammar and spelling.

Chinese characters remain the oldest writing system still in use. Their use was responsible for the invention of the fax machine in Japan, to facilitate handwritten communication, and continues thanks to the memory and versatility of the computer. The difficult period occurred before computers, since Chinese typewriters carried trays of some 2,000 characters which could be used in combination to produce a font of some 10,000 characters at an untrained speed of 2–3 characters per minute. Trained for three years, a typist could reach a speed of 20–30 which is not a bad comparison with the speed of western typing, if you think of a character as the equivalent of a word. But 10,000 characters is a limited number and typewriters were mainly used for very vocabulary-specific tasks, such as producing menus.

Chinese characters are known to have been introduced into Japan along with Buddhism by at least the early 6th century AD. From the 7th century the Japanese adopted them, terming them *kanji*, to write their own language which is, incidentally, totally different from the Chinese in terms of phonology and morphology. In order to express their own polysyllabic and agglutinative language, a set of phonetic symbols called *kana* was developed. These were to be used in conjunction with *kanji*: the latter for the meaning, and the former for inflectional ending, grammatical particles etc.

Since the end of the Second World War, the number of Chinese characters for general public use has been limited officially to some 2,000 *tôjô* or *jôyô kanji* (Chinese characters for daily or frequent use) which Japanese school children have been expected to master at the end of the 9th grade. However, learned and literary publications and other specialised areas such as names are free to exceed the government guidelines. Even with an addition of several thousand, the total number in normal use may seem far short of the 40,000 – 50,000 contained in larger Chinese dictionaries. What makes the Chinese characters such a formidable burden in reading and writing Japanese, however, is not the number but the complex and cumbersome way in which they are used. Unlike the monosyllabic Chinese language, most Chinese characters used in Japanese have a number of possible pronunciations depending on context. These sounds of *kanji*, called 'readings', are classified in two types: *kun* – the native Japanese pronunciation; and *on* – the approximations of the original Chinese sounds often referred to as 'Sino-Japanese' readings. A combination of *on* and *kun* has always characterised the Japanese use of Chinese characters.

In the 9th century, the Japanese simplified certain *kanji* to form two phonetic *kana* syllabaries: *hiragana* – 'smooth *kana*', a rounded flowing script derived from the cursive form of (whole) Chinese characters; and *katakana* – 'angular *kana*', a square type formed from the isolated parts of the characters. Each has forty-eight different signs plus diacritics. *Hiragana*, the more graceful of the two became the customary medium for the writing of personal correspondence and classical Japanese poetry and prose. Also known as *onnada* or 'women's hand', it flourished among the court ladies who wrote most great works of prose literature of the Heian period (794–1185), such as the *Tale of Genji*. The *katakana* system took on a subordinate role as an aid to reading Chinese texts and today it is most typically used for writing foreign words.

Since *kana* can express all the sounds of Japanese, the language can, in principle, be written entirely in *kana*. One of the obstacles to using *kana*, apart from the Japanese aesthetic preference for variation, is the extremely high rate of homophony (e.g. *ame*, can mean 'rain' or 'sweet'; or *ten* can stand for two completely different characters meaning 'sky' or 'dot' respectively). Therefore a mixture of Chinese characters and Japanese *kana* script known as *kana-majiri* has remained in general use to this day. The mix of cursive Chinese characters and the slender flowing line of *hiragana*, in particular, has enabled the Japanese to develop the art of calligraphy to the height of lyric grace (fig. 15).

Romanising Japanese presents few difficulties compared to languages with more ramified or intricate phonetic structures. However, the barriers to any large-scale conversion to romanisation are as great as those confronting the attempted wholesale use of *kana* referred to above. Apart from the cultural and psychological objections, romani-

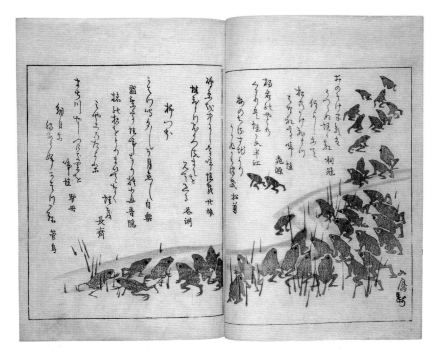

15. Japanese calligraphy, a combination of *hiragana* and *kanji*, most commonly used for writing Japanese. From *Shin kawazu awase*, an illustrated *haiku* anthology on the theme of frogs, woodblock colour printed, 1800.

BL, OIOC, Or. 81.c.11.

sation does not escape the pitfalls of ambiguity either. Nevertheless, romanisation has played a vital role in the computerisation of the Japanese written word. There is no longer a need to design a keyboard which displays even the minimum of 2,000 characters, as was the case with traditional typewriters. Characters are nowadays normally input by typing phonetically in the Latin alphabet and then selecting the appropriate *kanji* from the homophones displayed on the screen.

Indeed, Japan has been the leader in the Far East in tackling the manifold problems of handling Chinese characters electronically. As early as 1978, the Japanese National Bibliography was computerised by the National Diet Library. The problem posed today when exchanging information worldwide through the internet is less concerned with the range of Chinese characters involved than the standardisation of the different national character codes. Thus the handwritten document transmitted via fax retains a key role for the foreseeable future.

More than any other Eastern Asian language, Japanese has been infiltrated by foreign loan words (*gairaigo*), written in *kana* or Roman letters (*rômaji*). Approximately ten per cent of the Japanese language is thought to comprise *gairaigo*; and this ratio is increasing as Japanese

16. Japanese magazine cover using *kanji*, *katakana* and *rômaji* scripts and illustrating the new British Library building. *UK Weekly* (London, 1998).

lifestyles become ever more westernised. It is not uncommon, for example, to see advertisement signs in Japan written in a mixture of all four scripts: Chinese, *katakana*, *hiragana*, and *rômaji* (fig. 16).

Mixed systems (cuneiform and hieroglyphic)

Mixed systems are those which convey information through a combination of picture, idea and sound. Mesopotamian cuneiform script, which enjoyed a currency from *c.* 3,200 BC until the second century AD, is a good example of this (fig. 17). From the early pictographic base already mentioned, a system of abstract cuneiform signs had been developed by around 2,800 BC and was widely used for writing first Sumerian and then Akkadian (Babylonian and Assyrian). A new cuneiform script emerged in the Persian empire of Darius, around 500

BC, and continued in use until the second century AD, giving cuneiform a lifespan, from its origins, of nearly 3,400 years. The early pictographic form included some 2,000 signs, which were stylised to become a more linear script, largely because of the materials used, the reed stylus making wedge-like impressions on the clay. The practical considerations of working with these materials also seem to have influenced the transition from an early writing direction of vertical lines running from right to left, to horizontal lines reading from left to right. It is remarkable that the Mesopotamian cities came to an agreement on the hundreds of signs used, the initial plethora gradually reducing in number.

17. Sumerian cuneiform tablet. An administrative record of the late 3rd millennium BC.
BL, MSS, Add. MS 73519.

Cuneiform consisted of three main elements: pictograms, phonograms and determinatives. The pictograms could represent the Sumerian word for an object, an action associated with the object, or an idea associated with the object (e.g. 'sun' 'shining', or 'bright'). Phonograms represented syllables which could be used directly or like the rebus (a 'sounds like' substitution; for example, a disc could represent 'sun' or 'son'). Determinatives were signs which helped to clarify which sense was meant and to overcome ambiguity (e.g. a disc with a man would indicate 'son', rather than 'sun', as with Egyptian hieroglyphs).

Interestingly, although long-lived, the success of syllabic cuneiform was by no means compromised by its being freely adapted for use among unrelated languages, including adaptation from use with the Sumerian language to the Semitic language, to which its structure was less suited, spoken by the Akkadians from the first half of the third millennium BC onwards. It eventually gave way to the Aramaic script. Nonetheless, it was transmitted to the Elamites, Chaldeans, Hurrians and the Hittites of Anatolia (who borrowed the style of making signs with wedges, but not the cuneiform signs themselves and who also had their own hieroglyphic for display purposes) and formed the basis of Old Persian and Ugaritic. Nor was cuneiform restricted to practical, administrative uses; works of 'literature' also survive from as early as

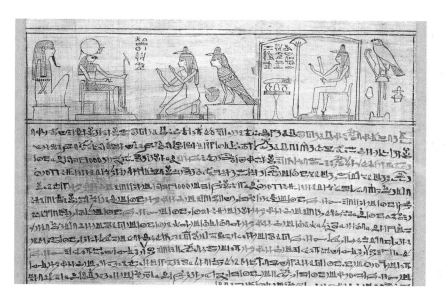

18. Funerary papyrus of the High Priestess Nesi-tanebtasheru, written in hieratic but with hieroglyphic captions. Thebes, 21st dynasty, *c.*950BC. The Greenfield Papyrus. BM, EA, 10554/5.

the third millennium BC onwards, with such highlights as the Epic of Gilgamesh and the law-code of Hammurabi, king of Babylon.

Egyptian hieroglyphic (figs 18–19) is another good example of a successful mixed system. Indeed, the appearance of a fully-fledged writing system in around 3,100 BC, just before the formation of Dynastic Egypt, has led to speculation on probable Sumerian influence, although pictograms from earlier Egypt do provide an indigenous background for some of the hieroglyphic symbols.

Egyptian hieroglyphs (from Greek *hieroglyphika grammata* – sacred carved letter) consist of a mixture of phonography (sound writing)

19. Diagram of Egyptian hieroglyphs from the diary of Thomas Young, who was instrumental in deciphering hieroglyphic, 1814–1829. BL, MSS, Add. MS 27281, f. 41.

25

and ideography (thought writing). Many symbols may be phonographic or logographic (indicating sounds or words), depending on context, and call for determinatives to clarify them. A symbol of an object might denote one particular word for that object (e.g. a drawing of a leg for 'leg'); an action might be expressed by its characteristic elements (e.g. a pair of legs for 'running'); or the symbol could have a phonetic value (e.g. a leg also = 'b'). The Egyptians did not generally mark vowels (our interpretation of pronunciation being heavily reliant upon later examples of the Egyptian language written in Greek or Coptic). They employed uniconsonantal, biconsonantal and triconsonantal signs, phonetic complements and determinatives/logograms. Determinatives are added at the end of phonograms to indicate the word's meaning where this is ambiguous (e.g. male and female figures to distinguish between lord and lady, or to determine the gender of names). Often one set of consonants could lend itself to many different words, or one word could have several different meanings, and determinatives are required to indicate which sphere of meaning is meant. To give a modern English example, a sign for the consonants 'bt' could stand for 'bite' (clarified by the determinative of a pair of teeth), 'bat' (clarified by either a cricket player or by a bat in a belfry) or 'beat' (clarified by a whip or a trophy). Phonetic complements are uniconsonantal signs, one or more of which may be added to a word to confirm its pronunciation or meaning (for example, by adding an 'r' or an 'm' to picture of a rodent, to confirm whether 'rat' or 'mouse' is meant).

The Egyptians had 26 single consonant signs including signs for 'i' and 'y', but not other vowel sounds. This engendered an ambiguity which meant that other signs had to be used to clarify meaning. Otherwise these phonetic signs could have been used, like the alphabet, for a purely phonetic consonantal script, but surprisingly the Egyptians chose not to develop this approach, perhaps because of the long history of sacred use of hieroglyphs, their prestigious status and elitist nature, or because they simply were not as difficult for contemporaries to understand as they are for us.

From hieroglyphic the Egyptians developed hieratic (Greek *hieratikos* – 'priest') and demotic (Greek *demotikos* – 'popular') scripts. These are essentially cursive (more rapidly written) versions of hieroglyphs, although in the speeding-up process some symbols become minimised or stylised, some new signs and abbreviations are intro-

20. Glyphs descended from those used by the Mayans, describing the history of the Mixtec people during the 11th cent. AD, in a manuscript on deerskin completed shortly before the Spanish conquest of Mexico. The Codex Nuttall. BM, Ethno., 39671,f.80.

duced and several hieroglyphs are merged into one sign. Hieroglyphs could be written vertically, horizontally, from right to left or left to right. Hieratic and demotic were consistently written from right to left and, invariably by the time of demotic, in horizontal lines. Hieroglyphs were well suited to formal display purposes, but were costly and time-consuming to produce. Hieratic seems to have been Egypt's everyday business script throughout, suited to production in ink by the reed pen (*calamus*) on papyrus. With the introduction of the yet more cursive demotic around 700–650 BC, hieratic became increasingly reserved for sacral purposes, with demotic becoming the pragmatic script 'in common use' by professional scribes, rather than being a script of the people as the name might suggest. Writing was still an elitist, professional preserve, confined to very few people.

Another mixed script system is that of Mayan glyphs (fig. 20), which are still undergoing decipherment following the renewed initiative of Valentinovich Knorosov (born 1922). The Mayan civilisation of Central America (modern Mexico, Guatemala and Belize, with parts of the Honduras and El Salvador) flourished between 500 BC and AD 1200 and produced 30 Mayan languages. Their complex number system (consisting of dots, bars and other graphic symbols, including a

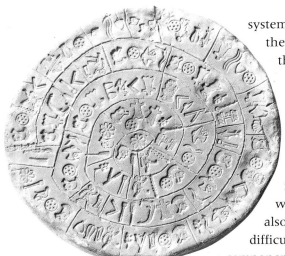

21. The Phaistos disc, Crete, 17th cent. BC? Cast, BM, G & RA, 1910.11–20.2 (original: Iraklion, Archaeological Museum).

The symbols, many of which are unparalleled, were punched with individual stamps, perhaps making it the earliest example of printing.

system of substitution by the faces of gods), suited to use in their complex theocratic calendrical calculations, was the first to be deciphered during the 19th century. However, from the time of Fray Diego de Landa (Bishop of Yucatan, 1572–9) and the Spanish Inquisition, it was realised that the Mayan glyphs were partly phonetic. The system combines phonography and ideography/logography. Mayan glyphs were even more unpredictable than Egyptian hieroglyphs, with the ability to write the same word in several different ways. Individual glyphs were also often combined (like Chinese characters), making it difficult to deconstruct these complex symbols into their component parts. The phonetic component was primarily syllabic, with some pure vowels, incorporating a quasi-alphabetic system but with more than one sign existing for some letters and also using syllabic signs.

Finally, another mixed script system is Rongorongo ('chants or recitations'), the undeciphered script of Easter Island in Polynesia, inscribed on wooden boards for recitation and consisting of some 120 stylised drawings of things and creatures (giving some 2,000 compound symbols). In all probability it was a form of proto-writing combining phonetic and logographic elements, like the very earliest Egyptian hieroglyphs, and with a largely mnemonic function. The origins of Rongorongo, which became defunct in the second half of the 19th century, remain obscure.

Phonography (sound writing): the phonetic systems (syllabic, consonantal and alphabetical)

Sound-based writing systems might appear to be more economic and efficient in the number of symbols needed, but they are language-based and require a double process of conversion, from idea to spoken language to graphic symbol, on the part of both author and audience. It is necessary to understand the spoken language and to recognise the symbols used. A system of reference is also required to establish that a word has a certain meaning according to its context, and in respect of spelling (orthography). To quote George Bernard Shaw's well-known example: 'fish' might equally well be written as 'ghoti' – 'gh' as in

'cough', 'o' as in 'women', 'ti' as in 'nation'. Phonetics alone are insufficient.

With these caveats in mind, phonetic script systems are perhaps best for conveying the nuances of language and the same symbols, or adaptations of them, can often be used within a linguistic group for several languages. During Antiquity signs were developed to correspond to sounds, representing either syllables of words, or smaller units of sound – letters. In the Semitic scripts these signs are mainly used for consonants with secondary signs indicating vowels. A Semitic group, the Phoenicians are thought to have carried this system to Greece and Italy, leading to the development of the alphabet.

22. Linear B, from Knossos, Crete, *c.*1400 BC.
BM, G & RA, 1910.4–23 (2).

Clay tablet carrying an inscription in Greek recording a gift of oil to the gods.

Ancient Mediterranean syllabic scripts

During the second millennium BC Crete formed a cultural focal point in the Mediterranean. The earliest Cretan script, found in short inscriptions on seal stones or rarely on clay, date to 2000–1500 BC A superficial resemblance to Egyptian hieroglyphs has led to it sometimes being called Cretan 'hieroglyphic'. Some 140 pictorial signs have been identified – too few for a developed pictographic or hieroglyphic system and probably indicating phonetic, syllabic use. By 1700 BC linear scripts were introduced. The first of these, Linear A (which remains undeciphered), reduces the signs to between 77–85 (scholarly opinion varies), still incorporating some pictorial signs but suggesting a primarily syllabic system. The Minoan language of this period is unknown, hindering decipherment of the Linear A clay tablets. Another puzzle is the Phaistos disc (fig. 21), dating to *c.* 1700 BC and allegedly discovered by workmen excavating at the palace of Phaistos in southern Crete. The 242 signs it carries were

23. Cypriot script, Akanthou, *c.*600–500 BC.
BM, G & RA, 1950.5.25.1.

Terracotta tablet carrying a Greek inscription in Cypriot script.

24. Spanish square Hebrew script, from the Barcelona Haggadah, Spain, mid-14th cent. BL, OIOC, Add. 14761, f.59v.

punched or stamped onto the clay (the first example of printing or typewriting?) and do not correspond to any of the other Cretan scripts, although some of its symbols are found on other artefacts, suggesting a missing link (or perhaps even a forgery).

With the coming of Mycenean influence between 1450 and 1200 BC Linear B (or 'Knossian court calligraphy'; *see* fig. 22) emerged as an adaptation to the new court language, Mycenean Greek. It has even been found on the Greek mainland at centres such as Pylos, Thebes and Mycenae. Like its Cretan forebears, Linear B seems to have been used primarily for accounting purposes. Half of its signs appear indebted to Linear A, and some to the early pictograms. The basic Linear B syllabary consists of 60 linear signs, with separate signs for each of the vowels and the remaining signs denoting a consonant followed by a vowel. As will be seen, its decipherment hinged upon the recognition that the language written was a form of Greek.

The first Cypriot script, Cypro-Minoan (fig. 23), relates to Linear A and similarly remains undeciphered. It contains about 85 syllabic signs and dates from around 1500 BC to the 12th century BC. From the 11th to the 3rd centuries BC a Cypriot syllabic script was used, employing 50 to 60 signs and featuring an early form of word separation by raised points or short strokes. It was used to write Greek and the unknown Eteo-Cypriot language; its points of resemblance to Linear B were a crucial factor in the recognition that the latter was also used for Greek, enabling its decipherment.

Consonantal and alphabetical scripts

The next major group to be considered are consonantal scripts. These consist primarily of the Semitic scripts (*see* figs 24–26) which fall into two main branches – North Semitic (including Phoenician, Aramaic, Hebrew, Syriac and Arabic) and South Semitic (including the North and South Arabian scripts, for example, South Arabian Sabaean and Ethiopic, and the scripts of Iran and Central Asia, for example, Sogdian and the Mongolian Uighur).

Consonantal scripts form a bridge between ancient syllabic scripts and the alphabet. They are essentially alphabetical in character, but solve the problem of indicating vowels in different ways. The Semitic Phoenicians are thought to have played a part in transmitting alphabetic principles to the West.

The cosmopolitan Semitic people of the eastern shore of the Mediterranean developed a consonantal script between 1800–1300 BC, but whether it was an independent invention or one inspired by an existing script system incorporating phonetic consonant signs (such as cuneiform, Egyptian or Hittite hieroglyphs, Cretan or Cypriot) remains hotly debated. Early Semitic scripts use 22 consonantal signs (Arabic script extends these to 29 and also grammatically and graphically rearranges them) and, as with Semitic languages, the meaning of a word is conveyed by consonants (usually three). Vowels play a secondary grammatical role, serving to clarify meaning according to context (for example, 'k-t-b/v' can mean 'book', 'to write', 'writer', 'I write', 'I wrote', 'script' etc., depending on the interpolated vowels). J and w came to represent the long vowels i (e) and u (o), with the glottal stop *aleph* for a. Another way of indicating vowels (found in Arabic and square Hebrew script) was to place dots (vowel points or *matres lectionis* from Latin 'mother of reading', what we think of as diacritics) above or below letters. Semitic scripts were written horizontally, generally from right to left.

The advantages of this adoption of an exclusively phonetic, consistent system are speed of writing and economy of space and materials.

25. Aramaic script, Elephantine, Egypt, 5th cent. BC.
BL, OIOC, Pap. cvi AB.

A story written in cursive Aramaic script on papyrus.

A theoretical disadvantage is that sound intrudes between thought and the way in which it is stored and retrieved – a knowledge of the language and how to articulate it is essential, for both author and reader. Writing had become what Malcolm Parkes has termed 'the written manifestation of substance of language'.

Semitic script, the first full, exclusive system of sound writing, became a powerful agent of information transmission in Europe and Asia. It was the vehicle for the preservation of the early texts of Judaism, Christianity, Islam, Hinduism and Buddhism and, with the spread of these cultures, achieved a long-lived international status.

The trading empire of the North Semitic Phoenicians, whose recorded history commenced around 1600 BC, played an important part in the dissemination of Semitic scripts. From its base in Syria and Lebanon the Phoenician network spread throughout the Mediterranean, its tentacles even apparently embracing far-off Cornwall. The Phoenician language belongs to the Canaanite Semitic sub-group, which includes Hebrew and the dialect of Moab. From the 13th to the 3rd centuries BC (and afterwards in its colonial Cypro-Phoenician and Carthaginian/Punic manifestations) it was written in the Phoenician (Semitic) consonantal script, which was primarily used for recording commercial transactions (*see* fig. 30).

26. Arabic script, from a Mamluk Qur'an, Egypt, AH 704 (AD 1304). BL, OIOC, Add. 22406, ff. 2v–3.

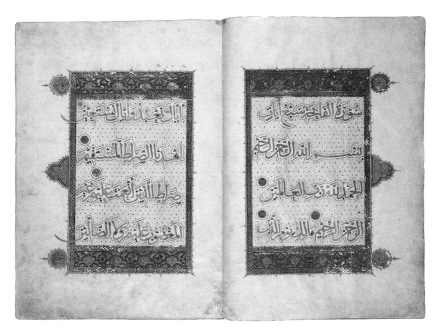

Among the many scripts which evolved from the Phoenician were the two Hebrew scripts, the first, Old Canaanite, used for religious literature and by the Samaritans, developing around the 9th century BC, and the second, the Jewish script or 'square Hebrew' (*see* fig. 24), dating from the 5th–4th century BC. Two other styles of script were used alongside square Hebrew, namely the intellectual 'rabbinic' and a cursive script.

Aramaic (*see* fig. 25), the official script of the Persian empire (eventually supplanting cuneiform) – the language spoken by Jesus Christ and used to write the Dead Sea Scrolls – also evolved from Phoenician script. It gave rise, in its turn (and via the Nabataeans of Petra), to Arabic (fig. 26) during the 4th–5th century AD. Two styles of Arabic script predominated: the monumental, angular Kufic script, used for copying the Qur'an and for display purposes until the 12th century AD; and the more cursive, rounded Naskhi, which underlies modern Arabic writing. Arabic remains, through the agency of Islam, one of the principal world scripts. It is also sometimes used for non-Semitic languages in Islamic areas and, as the Qur'an must be studied in Arabic, every Muslim should theoretically be literate in Arabic. The proscription of religious imagery in Islam has also meant that Arabic script has become the vehicle for sacred artistic expression, resulting in a high level of calligraphic artistry.

Perhaps due to the Persian conquest of the Indus region under Darius I, Aramaic seems to have generated one of the two oldest Indian scripts, Kharoshti (fig. 27). This enjoyed limited currency in north-west India and Central Asia from the 3rd century BC to the 3rd century AD (surviving sporadically in Central Asia until the 7th century AD). The second, Brahmi (fig. 28), is thought perhaps to have derived from a Semitic source. Nearly all of the ten contemporary

27. Kharoshti inscription, 2nd–3rd cent. AD. BM, Or. 8211/1682.

28. Brahmi inscription from a pillar carrying an edict of King Asoka, 3rd cent. BC. BM, Or. 1880–21.

One of the earliest examples of Indian script.

Indian scripts (as well as those of south-east Asia), apart from those imported by Islam, are descended from Brahmi which is used both for the Indo-European and Dravidian languages of North and South respectively. The earliest examples of Kharoshti and Brahmi occur on the northern Indian rock edicts of the Emperor Asoka (*c.* 270–232 BC).

Indian scripts have been variously described as alphabetical or an attempted conversion of a consonantal into an alphabetical system, but they are perhaps more properly considered syllabic or as a modified consonantal syllabary also known as an alphasyllabary. An advanced appreciation of phonology and grammar led to an ordered phonetic system, closely linked to pronunciation. In this the 44–52 basic signs (except for the Dravidian Tamil which has far fewer) are arranged according to the position of the letter in the mouth (vowels,

29. Ethiopic script, Hymnary, 18th cent. BL, OIOC, Or. 590, f. 101.

diphthongs and then seven groups of consonants – gutturals, palatals etc.). Consonants are considered syllabic, each containing a short 'a'. Consonants with no vowel following are combined as signs. Vowels can be written as independent signs if on their own or in an initial position, but are otherwise auxiliary signs (diacritics) written in relation to the consonant signs. Indian scripts generally run from left to right.

Thus Indian scripts, derived from a primarily consonantal Semitic base, developed phonetically along alphabetic lines to an essentially syllabic structure. Similarly the South Semitic Ethiopic script (fig. 29) also evolved from its consonantal base into a syllabic system – a reform often attributed to Indian or Greek influence, as is its method of reading from left to right.

The western alphabet

Alphabetic principles have already been touched upon in connection with many of the above-mentioned script systems, especially consonantal scripts which are essentially alphabetical in character. The groundwork was there, but who or what actually stimulated the development of the alphabet which underlies modern western scripts remains a mystery. Origins during the 2nd millennium BC amongst the Semitic slave-miners of Sinai, the cosmopolitan Canaanite traders of Lebanon and Israel, and in the caravan emporium of Ugarit in northern Syria (where frustration with Akkadian cuneiform seems to have resulted in the introduction of a 30-symbol cuneiform alphabet) have all been suggested. However, it is generally accepted that the early Greek alphabet was modelled on the 22 Phoenician consonant signs which were modified to become the Greek consonants and vowels (the weaker Semitic consonants of Phoenician becoming vowels), along with three new additional signs (*see* fig. 30). These were originally written from right to left, like Phoenician, or in a boustrophedon manner ('like an ox-drawn plough', back and forth, a form which appears every so often in different systems during Antiquity), but by the 5th century BC it had settled into a left to right direction. The ultimately pictographic ancestry of the characters is betrayed by the names of the characters themselves: Phoenician *aleph*/Greek *alpha* = ox/beef; Phoenician *beth*/Greek *beta* = house. The word *alphabet* (documented from the 3rd century BC onwards) literally means 'cowshed'.

		EGYPTIAN		PHŒNICIAN			GREEK							PELASGIAN		LATIN	
		HIERO-GLYPHIC	HIER-ATIC				Cadmean Right to Left	Left to right	LOCAL FORMS	EASTERN	WEST-ERN	LOCAL FORMS			LATIN	
a	eagle				alpha											a
b	crane				beta			M Melos etc. C Paros, Siphnos, Thasos, etc. L Corinth						B		
g	bowl				gamma			CC Corinth, Megara etc.			CC Chalcis, Locris, Arcadia, Elis, etc.				c
d	hand				delta											c d
h	plan of house?				epsilon			B Corinth, etc.							e
f, v	cerastes				digamma			[F]							f
ʼ (tch, z) duck					zeta									[G a new letter formed from C]	g
x (kh)	sieve				eta			H (hē)	H (h)					H	h
th	tongs; loop				theta										h
i	leaves				iota			Crete, Thera, Melos, Corinth, etc.							i
k	throne				kappa										k
l	lioness				lambda			L Attica L Argos			L Chalcis, Bœotia, etc.				l
m	owl				mu										m
n	water				nu										n
s	door-bolt				xi			H Later Argos [xi Attica, Naxos, Siphnos etc.]		[see below]					
ā	weapon				omikron			Ω Paros, Siphnos, etc. O, C Melos							o
p	door				pi										p
t (ts)	snake				san (ss)			M Halicarnassus, Teos, Mesembria							
q	knee?				koppa			[Q]							q
r	mouth				rho										r
š (sh)	field				sigma			Crete, Thera, M Melos, Argos, Corinth, etc.			M Phocis, etc.				s
t (tu)	arm with cake in hand				tau										t
	ADDED LETTERS:				upsilon										u, v
					xi			[see above]	X +						x
					phi										
					chi				X +	↓ Ψ					
					psi			[for Attica, Naxos, Siphnos, Thasos, etc.] ↓ Ψ		X Ozol.Locris, Arcadia.					
					omega			O Melos, Paros, Siphnos, etc.							
								[O used generally for g. έγω, etc. except in Ionia.]						Adopted at a late period as foreign letters. [Y / Z]	y / z

The Greek 'invention' of the alphabet (fig. 31) is thought to date somewhere between 1100–800 BC. As we have seen, the Greeks were familiar with Linear B and Cypriot, but do not appear to have used them widely. The earliest known alphabetic examples of writing in Greece (dating from the 8th century BC onwards) are for personal, quasi-literary rather than commercial use, leading to the unsubstantiated suggestion that the alphabet was developed as part of a move to record Homeric poetry. There is no corroboration for this in Greek tradition, but it is interesting to speculate that, although Homer himself would have composed and transmitted epics such as *The Odyssey* orally, if his followers did attempt to commit his legacy to writing (as was the case with Aristotle's students) there might be a cultural context for such invention. Parallel phenomena of the transition from an oral to a written culture, such as that faced by the Anglo-Saxons in the early 7th century AD, display a superficial similarity in borrowing and adapting or expanding the script of an influential neighbouring culture (in the case of the Anglo-Saxons, the adoption of the Roman alphabet with the addition of some ancient runic symbols of their own to cover sounds alien to Latin). An 'invention' of this sort cannot be ruled out, although background developments foreshadowing it must not be ignored.

The Ionian alphabet of classical Greece, authorised in Athens for documentary use in 403 BC, is that used in modern Greece. Another Greek alphabet – the Euboean – had earlier (around 750 BC) been

OPPOSITE:
30. Diagram showing the development of the alphabet: Phoenician, Greek, Etruscan and Roman.

From the Paleaographical Society, Series 2, pl. 101.

31. The Greek alphabet, from a Byzantine Gospel book made in Constantinople during the second half of the 10th cent., with images added during the second quarter of the 12th cent.
BL, MSS, Burney MS 19, ff. 101v–102.

(a)  (b)

32. The Phoenician (a) and Etruscan (b) alphabets on gold tablets from Pyrgi, *c.* 50 BC. Museo di Villa Giulia, Rome (Photo Scala).

introduced to Italy by Greek colonists and was adopted by the Etruscans and subsequently the Romans, forming the basis of the Latin alphabet. Due to the expansion of political and commercial empires such as those of the Romans, English, French, Spanish, Portuguese, Dutch and Americans, and to the influence of Christianity, the Latin alphabet has spread throughout much of the world.

The Etruscans of north and north-west Italy came under considerable Phoenician and Greek influence. In the 1st century BC they were absorbed into the Roman empire. They made extensive use of the Greek alphabet, but as the Etruscan language remains largely unknown their corpus of inscriptions can be read but not properly understood (figs 30 and 32). They were the intermediaries by which the alphabet was introduced to Roman society (fig. 33). Both the Etruscans and Romans made some modifications to the Greek Euboean alphabet, in accordance with their own phonetic requirements. These modifications continued in Europe during the Middle Ages, with the letters 'j' and 'w' being added and 'u' and 'v' becoming differentiated as separate letters, resulting in the modern 26-letter

Roman alphabet. This has required further modification in certain languages, such as French and German, which require accents and diacritics (such as the cedilla – ç) to convey different sounds.

The Greek (Ionian) and Roman alphabets were joined by Cyrillic script which has been used for over 60 languages (fig. 34). Its traditional inventor was St Cyril (*c.* 827–69) who was sent as a missionary to the Slavs by the Byzantine Emperor Constantine at the behest of King Ratislaw of Moravia. In order to convey Christianity in the Slav language Cyril appears to have devised the 40-character Greek-based Glagolitic alphabet. This prepared the way for the closely related early Cyrillic script, which originally had 43 characters but has been reduced to around 30 in modern Cyrillic scripts such as Russian. Other adaptations of the Greek alphabet include Coptic (used in Egypt from the 4th–9th centuries AD and perpetuated thereafter by the Coptic Church; *see* fig. 35) and the Armenian and Georgian alphabets ascribed to St Mesrob who was active during the early 5th century AD.

Two other non-Roman alphabets found in Europe are Germanic runes (*see* fig. 36) and Celtic ogham (*see* fig. 3). Academic understand-

ABOVE LEFT:
33. The Roman alphabet. Rustic capitals (main text), with annotations in a cursive half-uncial script in a copy of Terence's Fables (Codex Bembinus) copied in Italy, 4th–5th cent. AD. Vatican City, Bibl. Apost. Vat., Vat. Lat. 3226, f. LIV.

ABOVE RIGHT:
34. Cyrillic script, from a Russian writing master's roll, 1682–9.
BL, MSS, Add. MS 56073.

35. Coptic script, The Martyrdom of St Mercurius, Edfu, Upper Egypt, 985.
BL, OIOC, Or. 6801, ff. 1v–2.

ing of these was achieved through their occasional use in bilingual inscriptions alongside Latin script and through early medieval discussions of them in manuscripts. Limited knowledge of the early Germanic languages and ignorance of the Pictish language of much of early Scotland has somewhat hindered this. It has been suggested that both represent the responses of sophisticated oral societies to Greek and Roman scripts before adopting full literacy and the Latin alphabet, although the influence of pre-existing traditions cannot be ruled out. These peoples borrowed the idea of script and some letter-forms alongside others invented by themselves. The runic alphabet or *futhark* (after its first six letters) could uniquely be written in any direction, settling into left to right as time went on. Some of its letters are obviously related to the Roman (or more closely the Etruscan) alphabet, others represent distinctive Germanic phonetic elements, such as 'w' depicted by the character 'wynn' and 'th' depicted by 'thorn' (another character, 'eth' could also represent this sound in written Old English). The name 'rune' means 'secret', implying an origin in cult use or an elitist character, and their angular forms probably derive from being carved. The Old German runic alphabet (24 letters in three families of eight) is thought to have been used from AD 200–750. In Anglo-Saxon England the number of letters was eventually increased to 33 in response to phonetic demands. The later Nordic

1	2	3	4	5	6	7	8	9	10	11	12	13	14	15	16	17	18	19	20	21	22	23	24

ᚠᚢᚦᚨᚱᚲᚷᚹᚺᚾᛁᛃᛇᛈᛉᛊᛏᛒᛖᛗᛚᛜᛟᛞ

| f | u | þ | a | r | k | g | w | h | n | i | j | ï | p | z | s | t | b | e | m | l | ŋ | o | d |
| | | th | | | | | | | | | | | | R | | | | | | | ng | | |

36. Germanic runes.

ABOVE:
Diagram of the runic alphabet or *futhark* (Satwinder Sehmi after R. I. Page)

LEFT:
The Adoration of the Magi (right) and Weyland the Smith(left), from the Franks Casket, Anglo-Saxon Northumbria, first half of 8th cent. BM, M & LA, 1867.1–20.1.

runes, disseminated as far afield as Iceland and the Black Sea by the Vikings from around AD 800 onwards, decreased the characters to 16, hindering its coverage. In Christian societies runes could co-exist alongside Roman script for short inscriptions, and in Old English several runic characters were added to the Roman alphabet ('wynn', 'thorn', 'eth' and the æ diphthong 'ash'), but the use of runes gradually petered out after the 13th century.

Ogham (*see* fig. 3) or the 'tree alphabet' (its characters bearing the names of trees), which was mentioned above in connection with the oral tradition, resembles a tally in that it disposes horizontal or diagonal lines around a base-line (the vertical edge of a stone or stick). It was used by the Irish and in areas under Irish influence in western Britain between the 4th and 6th centuries AD, although its use may extend back into the Iron Age. Ascribed to the god Ogmios, it consists of 20 characters in families of five, suggesting that it may have derived from finger spelling, a practice used by compositors in printing, although the druidic interest in Pythagorian number symbolism might also play a role here. Vowels are distinctive in being denoted by a rising number of horizontal notches placed at right angles across the base-line. Ogham is used for short talismanic or commemorative

inscriptions and may have been developed by the druids, a professional priestly and learned class, for cryptic use, whilst preserving the
status of their well-disciplined oral tradition. It is interesting to note
that, although the characters do not resemble Roman letters, some
might represent exploded forms. For example, 'E' is written as four
lines. The same phenomenon occurs in the graffiti preserved at Pompeii – an 'E' is composed of four strokes, but who says they have to be
written as an upright and three horizontals, rather than as four parallel lines?

A superiority is often accorded unthinkingly to the alphabetical
system as it is economic in its use of symbols, can be written rapidly
and can be adapted to languages with widely different sounds and
grammatical structures. Whether there is in fact such a difference
between it and the consonantal and syllabic systems is a moot point,
as a study of origins and derivation has shown. Much of the world still
favours other systems, notably the consonantal Arabic, the syllabic
Indian and the ideographic Chinese. Nonetheless, the Roman alphabet continues to gain ground, bolstered by the growth of the English
language as the *lingua franca* of commerce and computing.

The creation of scripts to suit languages

St Cyril's invention of the Greek-based Glagolitic alphabet to enable
the use of the written vernacular in his mission to the Slavs during the
9th century is one example of the historical impetus to create a script
to suit a language. Christian missions had earlier necessitated this
process, however. Ulfila (*c.* 311–83), the 'Apostle of the Goths', left his
post as Bishop of Constantinople to return to the Goths of Moesia II,
beyond the limits of the Empire. Viewing language as an essential ele-
ment in conversion and wishing to translate the Bible into the Gothic
language, Ulfila invented written Gothic (fig. 37), drawing upon the
Roman and Greek alphabets. Similarly, within a decade of St Augus-
tine and his fellow Roman missionaries reaching Kent in 597 they had
apparently convinced the Anglo-Saxon King Æthelberht I that what
he most needed as a legitimate heir of Rome was a written law-code.
The preparation of this code (preserved in the 12th-century Textus
Roffensis) necessitated not only the introduction of a full system of literacy, itself no mean feat, but the invention of written Old English
(fig. 38), using the Latin alphabet with some additional characters

borrowed from the pre-existing but limited-use runic alphabet, as discussed above (*see* fig. 36). This raises the question of how much of the groundwork had already been achieved by the Germanic peoples with runes. The role played by the post-Roman British Church is also ambiguous in this respect. It is ironic that this early religious impetus to the development of the written western vernaculars should have given way to the bitter controversies surrounding later medieval/early modern attempts by Wycliffe, Tyndale and others to popularise the Bible by translating it into their own languages.

An East Asian example of an invented alphabet is Hangul, invented in Korea in AD 1443–6 under the sponsorship of a reforming ruler, King Sejong. The letter shapes of the consonants were based on observation of the positions of lips and tongue in producing the sounds. Such was the devotion of the Korean literati class to Chinese learning that the new 28-letter writing system was not universally welcomed, but it did enjoy popularity, particularly among women, until the end of the Choson dynasty in 1910. More recently, the communist government of North Korea abolished the use of Chinese characters in its publications in 1949, using Hangul exclusively, while in South Korea a mixed

37. Ulfila and the invention of Gothic script: the Codex Argenteus, Gothic Gospel book, Ravenna, 500–525. Uppsala, UB, DG I, f. 97.

38. Written Old English. The Vespasian Psalter, translation into Old English added around 820–40 to a Latin Psalter copied around 720–30, Canterbury. BL, MSS, Cotton MS Vespasian A.i, f. 53 (detail).

The oldest extant example of the translation of a biblical text into English.

39. Korean Hangul script.
Reprint of a 1446
woodblock printed book,
Seoul, 1946.
BL, OIOC, 16509.a.4.

script employing Chinese characters along with Hangul has persisted. Throughout the Korean peninsula, the Hangul alphabet is cherished as a symbol of national pride, being celebrated until recently in a South Korean public holiday, Hangul day.

A synthetic script which received a great deal of support, in this case from the Bible Christian Mission, was that invented in 1904 by Samuel Pollard and fellow missionaries to the non-Chinese Miao of south-west China (Miao script; *see* fig. 40). This consisted of geometric signs representing syllables and proved so successful that it was used for other non-Chinese dialects.

A late case of indigenous invention is that of the native American Sequoya who in 1821, with the assistance of his wife and child, devised Cherokee script (*see* fig. 41), largely by assigning syllabic values to the letters of the Latin alphabet and adding new symbols to form an 85-sign system. This initially enjoyed a high rate of success in instilling literacy amongst the Cherokee nation and is currently undergoing something of a revival.

Other North American examples include the Inuit scripts: Cree, invented by the English Methodist missionary John Evans in the 1840s and still used on Baffin Island; and the Alaskan script, invented by an Inuit Neck/Uyako (1860–1924) and helpers.

Deciphering and decoding scripts

How were many of these now defunct scripts first deciphered? The answer is invariably through a combination of hard work and luck. The capacity of the human brain for exploring intellectual teases is amply evinced by the passion for crosswords and other word-based games. The heroism of human intellect is demonstrated by the tireless work of the team of code-breakers who worked at Bletchley Park during the Second World War and is every bit as awe-inspiring as the physical acts of daring-do which are the substance of innumerable war-movies.

Prominent amongst the heroes of academic decipherment are: the diplomat Sir Henry Rawlinson, who risked life and limb to transcribe Darius's trilingual inscriptions on the rock faces of Behistun which played a crucial role in the decipherment of cuneiform; Jean François Champollion and Thomas Young, who were instrumental in cracking Egyptian hieroglyphs; and the English architect Michael Ventris (*see* fig. 42), who finally deciphered Linear B (building on work by the archaeologist Sir Arthur Evans, and by the American classicist Alice Kober).

Champollion's breakthrough with hieroglyphic came in 1823 and was crucially assisted by two monuments which carried bilingual

40. Miao script, St Mark's Gospel translated into Miao in the syllabic script invented by Samuel Pollard, printed in Shanghai, 1906. Courtesy of Albertine Gaur.

Cherokee Alphabet.

D *a*	R *e*	T *i*	ᕃ *o*	O *u*	i *v*
S *ga* O *ka*	F *ge*	Y *gi*	A *go*	J *gu*	E *gv*
ᕫ *ha*	P *he*	ᕬ *hi*	F *ho*	Γ *hu*	ᕗ *hv*
W *la*	ᕥ *le*	P *li*	G *lo*	M *lu*	ᕘ *lv*
ᕤ *ma*	O *me*	H *mi*	ᕙ *mo*	Y *mu*	
Θ *na* ᕵ *hna* G *nah*	Λ *ne*	ᕬ *ni*	Z *no*	ᕝ *nu*	O *nv*
T *qua*	ᕣ *que*	P *qui*	V *quo*	ᕞ *quu*	E *quv*
U *sa* ᕢ *s*	4 *se*	ᕫ *si*	ᕠ *so*	ᕬ *su*	R *sv*
L *da* W *ta*	S *de* ᕦ *te*	ᕬ *di* ᕬ *ti*	Λ *do*	S *du*	ᕬ *dv*
ᕬ *dla* L *tla*	L *tle*	C *tli*	ᕠ *tlo*	ᕬ *tlu*	P *tlv*
G *tsa*	V *tse*	ᕬ *tsi*	K *tso*	J *tsu*	C *tsv*
G *wa*	ᕬ *we*	O *wi*	ᕬ *wo*	ᕬ *wu*	6 *wv*
ᕬ *ya*	B *ye*	ᕬ *yi*	ᕬ *yo*	G *yu*	B *yv*

Sounds represented by Vowels.

a, as *a* in *father*. or short as *a* in *rival*. o, as *aw* in *law*, or short as *o* in *not*.
e, as *a* in *hate*. or short as *e* in *met* u, as *oo* in *fool*. or short as *u* in *pull*.
i, as *i* in *pique*. or short as *i* in *pit* v, as *u* in *but*, nasalized.

Consonant Sounds

g nearly as in English. but approaching to k. d nearly as in English but approaching
to t. h. k. l. m. n. q. s. t. w. y. as in English. Syllables beginning with g. except ᕦ have sometimes the
power of k. A. S. O. are sometimes sounded to. tu. ts. and Syllables written with tl except ᕦ
sometimes vary to dl.

41. Cherokee script, invented in 1821 by a
Cherokee, Sequoya. Courtesy of the American
Tourist Board and of Albertine Gaur

inscriptions in both Egyptian hieroglyphs and Greek: the obelisk at Philae and the famous Rosetta Stone (a trilingual priestly decree, also written in demotic script, discovered by Napolean's troops in 1799, forfeited to their English victors and now displayed in the British Museum; *see* fig. 43). These, along with earlier work by Thomas Young which Champollion did not acknowledge, provided the vital insight that the hieroglyphs contained phonetic as well as ideographic elements. This process of recognising components of the script revolved partly around noting repetitive elements, realising that some fulfilled an 'alphabetic' function, and isolating and identifying recurrent name forms (assisted by the Egyptian practice of setting names within linear surrounds known as cartouches).

The decipherment of Linear B hinged upon the isolation of recurrent groupings of three characters (Kober's 'triplets') which had different characters following them, suggesting a phonetic pattern and the process of declension in which words are given different endings (eg 'love', 'loves', 'loved'; 'Africa', 'African', 'Africans'). As a schoolboy Ventris had met Arthur Evans at a Minoan exhibition and determined to work on the script. He drew up grids based upon the frequency and regularity with which characters occurred on the tablets and then experimented by allocating them sounds and by

42. Michael Ventris, decipherer of Linear B (photo, Tom Blau, Camera Press, London).

guessing that some of the triplets represented Cretan place-names. In 1953, at the age of 34 and only shortly before his tragically early death in a car crash, Ventris realised, with the aid of Cypriot analogies and the discovery of a tablet at Pylos, that Linear B was used to record not the unknown languages of the Minoans and Mycenaeans (as Evans had believed) but an early pragmatic form of Greek. The key had been found.

It is salutary to note that some ancient scripts remain undeciphered, including definite writing systems, such as Indus Valley script and Proto-Elamite script, and symbols. Such are the enigmatic Pictish symbol stones of pre-9th century AD Scotland (fig. 44). The Picts, or 'painted ones' as Caesar called

43. The Rosetta stone: key to deciphering Egyptian hieroglyphic. BM, EA.

A trilingual priestly decree of 196 BC, in Egyptian and Greek, which was instrumental in the decipherment of Egyptian hieroglyphic.

them, have left a sophisticated archaeological record of complex dry-stone towers (brochs), fine metalwork and, above all, a large number of intriguing finely carved stones. The Picts seem to have been a fusion of indigenous prehistoric and Celtic Iron Age peoples who spoke an unknown pre-Indo-European language. This ignorance of language hampers the use of the Latin or ogham inscriptions, which appear on a very few of their works, in cracking their extensive series of picto-graphic symbols (mirrors, combs, crescents, 'z' and 'v' rods, snakes, 'dolphins'/Pictish beasts, horses, eagles, and so on). These are well developed and used in a consistent fashion, suggesting that they may convey messages of personal and tribal groupings and affiliations for memorials or boundaries; it has been speculated that their use on stones from perhaps as early as the 1st century AD may have been preceded by a system of personal tattooing.

Cryptography (Greek *kryptos* – hidden, *graphein* – to write) has a long history. Runes and other secret or elitist scripts have already been mentioned. Ciphers and codes are instrumental. The Egyptians used ciphers to convey secret military orders, a practice adopted by the Romans and made a common feature of modern warfare and politics since the time of the Machiavellian Renaissance courts. Ciphers essentially consist of the substitution or transposition of a unit (a letter or group of letters) with other letters or symbols, but without a change in sequence (e.g. that which Suetonius says was used by the Emperor Augustus which substituted the following letter of the Roman alphabet, thus 'sea' becomes 'tfb'). Codes involve the substitution of different elements (for which a key is necessary) for elements of varying kinds (letters, words, sentences, phrases, numbers and so on). Technology has been used increasingly in breaking such devices, since the introduction of the first cipher machines around 1925.

44. Pictish symbol stone, Aberlemno roadside I, 6th or 7th cent. AD ?, NE Forfar, Scotland.

The symbols are a serpent, a double disc and z-rod and a mirror and comb. They may record someone's gender, rank and tribal affiliations.

Form and function

Whichever form of writing is favoured, the shapes of its symbols and the way in which it is written will be moulded by the materials used and the purpose for which it is employed. It has not been generally considered appropriate throughout much of the history of writing, especially in the West, to use the same grade of script for a shopping list as for prestigious religious or literary texts. Some scripts will involve a high degree of care and will be formal or 'set', with many separate actions of the writing implement being required to produce their characters. Others will be written more rapidly and with greater economy of time, effort and materials and will accordingly be 'cursive' or, at the lowest end of the spectrum, 'current'. The 'aspect' of a script is its overall appearance and its 'ductus' the way in which it is written (the way in which the characters are formed and

45. Palm leaf manuscript, Bhaktapur, Nepal, 1549. BL, OIOC, 14325, ff. 1v-2.

relate to one another, the number of strokes used and the care and speed exerted in production). As script systems develop they often come to include an hierarchical gradation of scripts. This has already been seen in the case of carved Egyptian hieroglyphs which came to be written with a reed pen in the more formal hieratic and the cursive demotic forms. The Roman alphabet has been used in the West for a vast tree of scripts, the evolution of which has frequently been affected by technology and history.

46a. Egyptian papyrus scroll.
BM, EA, Pap. 10748.

Technology does not exist in a vacuum, but often develops in response to a perceived need or to historical circumstances. This is equally true of the technology of graphic communication, however much Information Technology may sometimes seem to be setting its own agenda and driving its own development. A study of the many and varied ways in which people have communicated over the centuries should assist us in discerning underlying constant factors, requirements and difficulties and allow us to rationalise what we expect of today's electronic technology, as well as enriching our exploration of its potential, discovering what it is best used for (and not) and broadening our horizons. We have to understand our place in the transmission and processing of knowledge across time and space, otherwise we run the risk of information overload and of developing communication indigestion.

The technology of writing and the materials used

Over the centuries (especially with more widespread literacy introduced from the time of the Roman Empire) human beings have written on most things. They still do – beer mats, plaster casts for broken limbs, walls... The materials used will often influence the appearance of a script: cuneiform means wedge-shaped, reflecting the shape of the impressions made on clay by the square end of the reed stylus. The angular form of Roman square capitals was influenced by the use of the chisel and the more fluid rustic capitals by the use of a reed or quill pen. Materials can also dictate the form of a document (figs 46a and b): papyrus is suited to rolling as a scroll, not to folding as a book, and palm leaves will dictate an oblong format (*see* fig. 45).

46b From scroll to codex, and back again (cartoon, Phil Healey, briefed by Michelle Brown).

The ancient scroll presented problems of portability and cross-referencing. The early Christians favoured the new codex or book form. With electronic searchability, we are returning to the scroll on our pcs, but there are still times when only the book will do.

Bone, stone, wood and clay (as tablets, bricks, pots, pot sherds or *ostraka* etc.) were popular early writing supports. Most metals have also been used, from bronze for Roman military diplomas to gold for Etruscan plaques and Balinese official letters. Bamboo, bark and palm leaves, materials widely used in south and south-east Asia, have also been popular. From around 3,000 BC the Egyptians used the sedge plant papyrus (*see* fig. 46a) to make a support sheet by cutting its stem into strips, overlaying them criss-cross fashion and beating them until they were fused together by their own sap and then polishing the surface with pumice. Islamic expansion from the 7th century AD onwards cut off most of the Mediterranean sources of papyrus, although Sicily and Syracuse continued as sources and the papal chancery continued to use it sporadically as an exotic item until the 11th century. Theoretically it could be washed and reused (palimpsested), but the archaeological discoveries of large archival dumps indicate that it was widely enough available in Antiquity for this generally not to have been necessary.

Perhaps the most long-lived and effective forms of writing support materials have proven to be: the reusable wax tablet (wooden tablets carrying recesses inset with beeswax which could be inscribed with a pointed stylus of metal or bone, the triangular end of which might be used to erase and to smooth the wax; *see* fig. 47); parchment or vellum (prepared animal skins – sheep or goat for parchment and calf for vellum; *see* fig. 48); and paper (formed of pulped organic materials; *see* fig. 53). These have now been joined by film and by the digital disk,

the archival and commercial shelf-life of which are, as yet, unknown (although a cautious ten-year lifespan for CD-ROMs is favoured in some preservation circles).

Wax tablets (the *tabula, tabletta* or *ceraculum;* fig. 47) were used continually from the time of the Assyrians and Egyptians until the 19th century, when the fishermen of Dieppe still used them to record their catches. They were used in the schoolroom (until replaced by slates and chalk) and at university lectures, as Roman passports, as notebooks and 'filofaxes', love-tokens, temporary and permanent accounts (favoured for medieval French royal household accounts),

47. A wax tablet used for a schoolboy's exercises, N. Africa, 2nd cent. AD. A metal or bone stylus was used to write on the wax, revealing the white surface on the underlying wooden tablet. The top two lines were probably written by the tutor (a quote from the poems of Menander written in Greek uncial script) and the pupil has copied below, cheating by running onto the frame.
BL, MSS, Add. MS 34186 (1).

48. Parchment: the Codex Sinaiticus, Caesarea, 4th cent. AD.

BL, MSS, Add. MS 43725, ff. 244v–245.

With the edicts of toleration of the 4th cent. Christianity became popular and promoted the production of the parchment codex, as in this luxurious copy of the Bible in Greek uncial script. The unusual use of 4 columns is a vestige of the layout of a scroll. 1–2 columns soon became the norm for the codex.

liturgical aids, notice-boards and so on. They were frequently used in dictation and for drafting texts and, like their electronic counterparts, as draft texts were often not retained, thereby restricting our knowledge of the authorial/editorial process. In some respects they fulfilled the function of the modern lap-top computer.

The invention of parchment/vellum (the terms are often used interchangeably and generically, as well as specifically) is ascribed, according to tradition, to the rulers and librarians of Pergamum (Bergama in modern Turkey), whence it derived its early name – *pergamenum*. A trade embargo by Egypt, the principal source of papyrus, during the 2nd century BC allegedly led to experimentation in Pergamum with animal skins as a writing support. The resulting material was rather leather-like and did not really catch on until the rise of the codex or book form from the 4th century AD and refinements in production which led to parchment/vellum proper (*see* fig. 48). This was made by soaking the skins in a bath consisting predominantly of lime, stretching it on a frame, dampening it and scraping it with a lunular (crescent-shaped) knife until it reached the required thickness. The thinner the sheet the greater the difference in appearance between the whiter, velvet-like flesh side and the yellow, smoother hair side (which can also display speckled hair follicles). The method of prepa-

54

ration varied somewhat according to time and place. The Insular
world of the Celts and early Anglo-Saxons, for example, favoured a
thicker, suede-like form with little hair/flesh contrast. The Caroli-
gians, like their Roman predecessors whom they sought to emulate,
preferred a thinner, differentiated material, leading to differences in
the way in which leaves were assembled in the book so that like
would face like at an opening. The differences in manufacture play as
great a role in the differing appearance of parchment (sheep or goat)
and vellum (calf) as the animals used and it is often extremely difficult
to tell one from the other unless hairs remain adhering to the edges of
holes (caused by insects biting the beasts and causing weak spots
which open during the stretching process). Materials were so precious
that such blemished skins were widely used. Sometimes sheepskins
were split along the epidermis to form two thin sheets and occasionally, especially during the Renaissance, uterine vellum from stillborn
calves is thought to have been used for a particularly fine white surface. Whitening agents such as chalk were added during stretching
and the finished sheets were smoothed with pumice and cut to size
(folio, quarto or octavo, like paper, according to how many times they
were folded). The finished sheet is called a bifolium. When making a

49. Papyrus scrolls and a
capsa for storage, from the
Vergilius Romanus,
written in rustic capitals,
Rome, second half 5th
cent. AD.
Vatican City, Bibl. Apost.
Vat., Vat. lat. 3867, f. 3v.

codex these are folded in half to produce folios or leaves and assembled into gatherings (or quires).

Papyrus scrolls (the *rotulus; see* figs 46, 49 and 50) written on with a reed pen (*calamus*) were used, alongside the wax tablet, for literary and other longer texts in Graeco-Roman Antiquity. The practice of binding several wax tablets together with leather thongs to form booklets may have inspired experimentation with the book or *codex* form (from Latin *caudex* = tree bark), initially employing thin sheets of wood or papyrus, which was inclined to split when the sheets were folded into a book. As early as the 1st century AD the Roman poet Martial urged his readers to favour the more convenient codex form, but it remained a little-used, cheaper form, chiefly popular among 'low life' such as the underground Christian movement. The attraction of the codex was allegedly its portability, handy during times of persecution, although this may have been over-estimated given the size and weight of some of the larger tomes. Its popularity perhaps owed more to its iconic Christian status and to a conscious publishing drive. It also carried the benefits of easy cross-referencing from one part of the text to another. If one were popping off to Ostia Antica for a little holiday and wanted to take some light reading, say in the form of Ovid's *Metamorphoses*, one would need to take several *capsae*, resembling Victorian hat-boxes, full of papyrus scrolls (*see* fig. 49). Heaven help one if one wished to compare favourite passages and had to locate them in the various scrolls. Only now, with the aid of electronic searchability have we returned to extensive use of the scroll mechanism on our computers. The scroll did survive Antiquity, however, and in fact a large quantity of the writing of the medieval West survives in scroll form, through its continued use for retaining large bodies of administrative data, such as Exchequer rolls. Scrolls were also often used for display purposes such as illuminated royal genealogies, and for liturgical functions such as the Italian Exultet rolls, used in the Easter liturgy and adapted for simultaneous reading of text and image by deacon and people by having the pictures upside-down to the text so that the congregation could 'read' them as the roll was fed over the lectern. In

50. Hebrew scroll carrying the Book of Esther in a Sefardi hand, on 3 strips of vellum of approx. 6 x 5 cm each on an ivory roller. 17th cent. BL, OIOC, Add. 11831.

Judaism the scroll retained a prominent role, and is used for preserving the sacred *Torah* (fig. 50).

When Christianity emerged from underground, with the edicts of toleration of the 4th century, the codex came with it and began to be used for luxurious editions of the Bible, such as the Codex Sinaiticus (*see* fig. 48). The preparation of parchment/vellum had been perfected by this time and the new books were made of this remarkably durable material. During the publishing revolution which ensued, as scrolls were copied in codex form, a great many works of Antiquity were lost, being deemed unworthy of the new 'reprints' or otherwise commercially unviable by the professional publishers who were a feature of Roman urban life. A similar phenomenon of censorship and selection was faced during the transition to print culture in the West during the 15th to 16th centuries, and is being faced again now as it becomes apparent that not everything can be kept. Our copyright libraries are sinking under the weight of information, much of it produced in an ephemeral form on poor-quality acidic wood-pulp papers (introduced with the explosion of literacy in the late 19th century). The choices of what to preserve (often a costly business), what to copy onto microform or electronic disk (entailing a rolling programme of perpetual recopying for purposes of archival retention which embraces millions of items) and what to let go are difficult and often emotive.

The stylus, the reed pen and its eastern bamboo counterpart were joined during the 6th century by the introduction of the flexible quill pen (*penna;* often a goose's flight feather), ideally suited to the parchment surface, which completed the technological revolution. The inks used from this time, and throughout the Middle Ages, were made primarily of lampblack or gall. The lampblack was carbon, produced, for example, by placing a silver bowl over a candle and scraping off the soot, then mixing with water and gum. The caustic liquid gall was extracted from oak galls which are formed when an insect stings the twigs to lay its eggs, producing a small apple-like berry. The Latin name for ink, *encaustum* – 'burnt in', reflects the way in which gall etched into the parchment. This colourless substance was mixed with iron salts, the ferrous ink so produced often fading to brown over time, although some lampblack was also sometimes added. From the 15th and 16th centuries copper-based inks, which fade to grey/green, also occurred. The industrial revolution led to the introduction of manufactured chemically-based inks in the 1830s (with aniline dyes

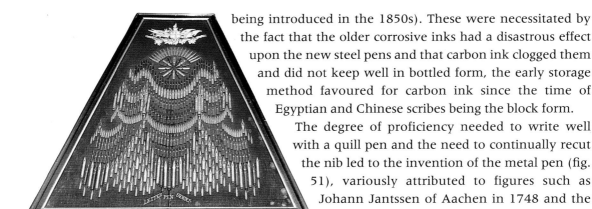

51. Steel pen nibs, arranged as an advertisement for the leading Birmingham manufacturer, Mitchell's, second half 19th cent. Courtesy of Philip Poole, 'His Nibs'.

being introduced in the 1850s). These were necessitated by the fact that the older corrosive inks had a disastrous effect upon the new steel pens and that carbon ink clogged them and did not keep well in bottled form, the early storage method favoured for carbon ink since the time of Egyptian and Chinese scribes being the block form.

The degree of proficiency needed to write well with a quill pen and the need to continually recut the nib led to the invention of the metal pen (fig. 51), variously attributed to figures such as Johann Jantssen of Aachen in 1748 and the American Peregrine Williamson in 1800. Nibs of horn or tortoiseshell embedded with precious stones and gold were tried, but steel nibs on wooden, uncut quill or elaborate carved or jewelled holders were found to come closest to the action of a quill. From the late 1830s fountain pens with reservoirs made an appearance, becoming widespread from the end of the century (with American based firms such as Parker and Waterman initially heading the field). Birmingham became the centre of the steel-nib trade, boasting firms such as Mitchell's, and by the end of the century was producing over 175 million nibs per annum, by means of predominantly female sweated labour. Printing and the educational explosion of the later 19th century (especially following the Education Act of 1870) had impacted upon mass literacy and industry supplied it with the pens and the cheap machine-made papers needed to fuel it. More people were writing than ever before. The new nibs were suited to the linear needs of copperplate, an engraved script popularised by the printed instruction manuals and copybooks of the writing masters (such as that of George Bickham whose influential *Universal Penman* had appeared in 1733–41). Translated into mass terms this ultimately led to cursive tendencies in script, aggravated by the 'invention' of a version of the ball-point pen in the 1940s by a Hungarian refugee to Argentina, Laszlo Biro. This has contributed to something of a degeneracy in modern western handwriting, despite the gallant attempts of Benjamin Franklin Foster and Platt Rogers Spencer who advocated good writing practice for business use, and of calligraphers such as Edward Johnston (the 'father of modern calligraphy' and inventor of the foundational hand), and Alfred Fairbank (reviver of italic handwriting) to arrest this process of deterioration.

Further mention should be made of some popular modern writing implements. The modern pencil is descended from the ancient lead-point (a thin piece of lead in a holder), with graphite being introduced from the mid-16th century. The ball-point pen was experimented with from the late 19th century (J. J. Loud patented a prototype in 1888). A metal ball-bearing revolves in the mouth of the pen and is fed with ink by gravity or capillary action. Ink can also be stored in an absorbent material, as with 20th-century fibre-tip pens, which differ little in principle from the reed brush of Antiquity. Experiments by Thomas Edison and others during the later 19th century with electric pens, working on a stencil principle to duplicate graphic marks, led to David Gestetner's wheel pen and drum duplicator (patented 1905) and the photocopier, developed from 1907 onwards. Precursors of the typewriter are known from the early 18th century onwards, but the American Christopher Latham Sholes patented the 'typewriter' proper in 1868, joined by Thomas Edison's electronic typewriter patent of 1871.

52. A medieval illuminated manuscript, La Somme le Roy, illuminated in Paris in the late 13th cent. by the famous illuminator Maître Honoré.
BL, MSS, Add. 54180, ff. 136v–137.

We know something of the composition of inks and pigments used during the Middle Ages (*see* fig. 52) from technical tracts such as the *De Clarea* and the *De Diversis Artibus* of the monk Theophilus (thought to have been writing in Germany around 1100) and from artists' model-books, such as the 15th-century Göttingen modelbook, which give samples of pigment alongside recipes. Modern reconstruction of early pigments and current programmes of analysis using raman lasers have greatly enhanced this knowledge. Pigments consisted of animal, vegetable or mineral extracts added to beaten egg-white (*clarea* or glair) as a binding agent to hold it to the page. They were applied with an animal-hair brush (squirrel hair was often used), or a pen if their viscosity permitted. Popular early medieval pigments included local plant extracts, such as gorse, lichens and irises for yellows and sap greens, blue from the indigo or woad plants, or a remarkably versatile purple from folium (turnsole – *crozophora tinctoria*) which could vary from a red to a blue purple depending on the addition of acidity (for which stale urine was a favoured source) or alkalinity. The highly prized purple of Antiquity extracted from the murex mollusc (from which the Greeks thought the Phoenicians derived their name) does not appear to have been much used in the early medieval West, or indeed in Byzantine illumination, despite Bede's reference to its manufacture from the dog whelk in Anglo-Saxon Northumbria. Mixed or organic purples such as folium, or a pink called kermes made from crushed insects, seem to have predominated. Some substances found in what are wrongly considered remote areas (such as the island of Lindisfarne off the north-east coast of England, where the Lindisfarne Gospels was probably made around 700) are exotic in origin, notably the deep blue known as ultramarine, its name indicating the source of its base, lapis lazuli, across the sea in Persia and Afghanistan. This affords us a glimpse of the trade routes into which this centre must ultimately have tapped. The mineral azurite was another popular source of blue and malachite of green, for which verdigris was also used, made, for example, by suspending a piece of copper over vinegar and scraping off the green corrosive substance formed. In addition to earth colours and ox-gall used for yellow, there was orpiment, a trisulphide of arsenic, which gives a vibrant bright yellow sometimes used in place of gold. The red minium (from which 'miniate', and 'miniature' are derived) was initially made of cinnabar, mined by the Romans in Spain, and although it was artificially manufactured from mercury during the Middle Ages as vermilion, the term minium was gradually applied to the more common red lead (toasted lead). The use of red ink to highlight titles, headings and instructions within the text also gave rise to the term 'rubric' from *rubeum* – red. Red lead, and its white and yellow mates, often oxidise over time and turn white to black to silver, sometimes misleading the viewer into thinking that passages of text were written in silver. This was sometimes used, although much less commonly than chrysography (writing in gold), but usually it is oxidised red lead.

A change in palette occurred during the 14th century, with the rise of experimental science and the growth of the cloth trade. Artificially created substances such as copper blues and new organic sources such as timber extracts (for example, brazil wood imported from Ceylon) were tapped to produce the 'red lakes', and saffron and other plants were exploited for their yellow and green dye-stuffs. The influence of cloth-dying is reflected in the illuminator's use of clothlets, pieces of cloth impregnated with a dye which was released upon soaking. The old favourites also remained, with later medieval town ordinances taking steps against the woad growers, for example. Woad is an all-growth feeder which leaves the soil barren for several generations and which cut swathes across Europe's agricultural land in a manner that was already causing concern in Charlemagne's day (around 800). Woad also smells unpleasant when boiled to release its dye, hence the concern of medieval town-dwellers to ensure that such activities were kept outside 'city limits'.

Another mainstay of the manuscript painter or 'illuminator's' art was gold, the terms 'illuminate' and 'illumination' deriving from the Latin *illuminare* – to light up (*see* figs 55–59). It could be applied as an ink in a costly powdered form, but this seems only occasionally to have been used for fine detailing. The usual method of application was as gold leaf. It has been estimated that a cubic square inch of this finely beaten gold would be enough to gild a football pitch, although this has yet to be tested. The gold leaf was laid over an adhesive substance laid on the page, such as fish glue, gum (either from animal horn or from a plant such as the acacia for gum arabic) or, commonly during the high Middle Ages from the 13th century onwards, on top of a raised bole – a plaster-like mixture (gesso), often coloured red, to which the gold adhered with the aid of moisture from the artist's breath. Once laid, the gold had to be brushed or trimmed off to remove the excess and was then usually burnished, that is polished, with an agate, a dog's tooth or another smooth implement until it shone. It might also be tooled – patterned – with the use of tools such as styli or punches. Even whole texts written in gold (chrysography) could be written in this way. Silver could also be used, but was less common, perhaps because it is prone to oxidisation and turns black. A messy process, gilding was often the first stage in illumination.

The art of illumination survived the advent of printing in the West during the second half of the 15th century. Many of the more luxurious early printed books ('incunables') contain hand produced illumination (*see* fig. 54) and the practice continued, alongside calligraphy (from the Greek for 'beautiful writing'), for the production of fine books and works of art. Both calligraphy and illumination are still widely practised throughout the world.

Parchment/vellum was used for some early printed books, but was rapidly overtaken by paper (*carta, charter; see* fig. 53) which is formed from pulped organic substances. The Chinese had used silk and other cloths as writing surfaces since the Zhou dynasty and developed the cheaper alternative of paper through pulping cloth, bamboo or mulberry bark. Though the invention is traditionally ascribed to the eunuch Cai Lun who reported on paper-making to the Emperor in AD 105, paper fragments dating back to the 2nd century BC have been excavated in sites in the Gobi desert. In the 8th century the Islamic governor of Samarkand is said to have extracted the manufacturing technique from Chinese captives. The process spread throughout Islamic territory and was transmitted via areas of cultural overlap, such as Spain and Sicily, to the West. Paper was made in Muslim Spain from the late 11th century and in Italy from the 13th century. In the 14th to 15th centuries manufacture spread to Switzerland, the Rhineland and France. Rather as with the early codex, paper was initially used for low-level pragmatic literacy, such as letters, merchants' accounts and notaries' registers. The earliest English paper documents are the early 14th-century borough registers of King's Lynn and Lyme Regis. However, England did not manufacture paper until the 15th century, and then only half-heartedly until the mid-16th, Caxton and other early printers importing their supplies from the Continent.

These early papers were made from cotton or linen rags which were pulverised and pulped by soaking in vats of water and size until they

achieved the consistency of liquid latex. Moulds consisting of wires (horizontal lines, used to guide writing, being termed 'laid lines' and their vertical supports 'chain lines') in a wooden frame (the Chinese had used a bamboo mesh) were then dipped in the substance and agitated until it began to set and the fibres meshed. These wires often incorporated 'brand' symbols known as watermarks (ox heads, crowns, monograms and the like). Identification of the watermarks

53. Paper used in a Persian manuscript, a poetical anthology in 'Turkman' style, Shemakha, AH 873 (AD 1468). BL, OIOC, Add. 16561, ff. 59v–60.

The flooding of Baghdad. Islam introduced coloured papers, sometimes flecked with gold and glazed.

63

can assist in dating a paper manuscript (bearing in mind the time lag that might occur between production, sale and use) and locating its possible paper source. The sheets of paper were then turned onto felt blotting sheets between boards, and pressed. The paper so produced is remarkably tough and does not present the same problems of preservation as its acidic wood fibre counterparts, which have been in widespread use as primary materials or additives since the 1860s. Acid-free papers have continued to be produced for higher-grade use and are now becoming more widespread.

Paper was used for lower-grade books from around 1400 and for some legal documents from the 16th century. It rapidly became the usual support for the printed word. Graphic communication produced with the aid of stamped impressions has a long history. Bricks from the time of Nebuchadnezzar (6th century BC) carry stamped imprints. To the Chinese again belongs the credit for the technological innovation of printing works with woodblocks, a famous early example of a full printed work being the Diamond Sutra from Dunhuang, a Buddhist prayer scroll which dates to AD 868, although woodblock printing was known in the East for at least a century before this. Moveable type followed, being introduced via China and refined in Korea during the 14th and 15th centuries. It was introduced to the West by the German Johannes Gutenberg with the printing of the Gutenberg Bible in 1455 (fig. 54). This started a new revolution in information transmission which is only now being rivalled by the electronic age.

The early printed books (incunables, from the Latin *in cunabula* – 'in the cradle'/'origins') used manuscripts as their exemplars. They were influenced by their mise-en-page (layout) and the way in which they articulated text with the use of decoration and different scripts or coloured inks, as well as by handwritten scripts which were used as the models for early typefaces (Gothic script being favoured in northern Europe and those of the humanists inspiring the Veneto-Roman and italic typefaces in Italy). Printed books also initially featured illumination by hand. Conversely, 15th to 16th-century manuscripts sometimes include woodblock illustrations (and are known as xylographs). The transition from manuscript to print was gradual and evolutionary, not a total break, and printing by no means rendered handwriting redundant. The two forms have, throughout their history, interacted in accordance with an approach to form and function

54. From manuscript to print: the '42-Line Bible', printed by Johannes Gutenberg in 1455. BL, PB, C.9.d.3,[a], f. 5.

A landmark in printing history: the earliest example of the use of moveable type in the West.

in which handwriting has continued to function for informal and portable contexts, at various stages in the authorial and editorial processes, and for fine book production and artistic uses. Departments of manuscripts (*manu* – hand, *scriptos* – written) in modern libraries include not only items written in Antiquity and the Middle Ages, but items penned (or even typed) yesterday or today.

THREE

Writing in the West

Making a medieval illuminated manuscript: techniques and stages of production

This 13th-century German manuscript (Copenhagen, Königliche Bibl., MS 4, 2°), juxtaposed with images of a modern calligrapher at work, illustrates some of the processes involved in writing and illuminating a medieval book (*see* figs 55–59).

1. Skins are soaked in alum and lime, stretched on a frame, scraped whilst damp and whitened (e.g. with chalk) to make parchment (sheep or goatskin) or vellum (calfskin).

2. The scribe obtains the prepared skins from a parchmenter.

3. The parchment is cut to size and pricked with a stylus or an awl and ruled to establish the layout of text and image, sometimes with the aid of a template (hard-point was initially used for ruling and was joined by lead-point in the late 11th century and ink in the late 13th century).

4. Whilst ruling-up the scribe has to work out how many words there are to a page, imposing the text like a typesetter, for the pages are not written out in the order in which they will be read because the bifolia will have to be folded (thus a scribe working on a standard quire of four bifolia to be folded into a quire of eight leaves will write the text of its last and first pages on the first bifolium to be laid out in front of him or her).

5. The scribe writes on a double sheet (bifolium). Several of these will be folded together to form a gathering (quire). The finished quires will eventually be sewn together to form the book.

6. The scribe cuts the quill pen to form a nib. It has to be trimmed to sharpen the nib every page or so.

7. Having tested the pen on a spare scrap of parchment, the scribe is now ready to begin writing.

8. The scribe holds a pen-knife in the other hand to steady the parchment and to maintain even hand pressure.

8a. Corrections might be made by erasing with a knife, by scoring out or by expunctuating (indicating erroneous elements by putting dots beneath them).

8b. The parchment's surface is restored with sandarac (or pounce, a powdered conifer resin).

9. The scribe may leave guide-letters to instruct the artist what to paint and would normally mark the quires in some way (quire numeration, quire signatures or catchwords) to assist in assembling them into a book – work proceeded too quickly to stop and read the text. After the scribe finished work the rubricator (often the same person) added the rubrics (titles and so on) in red and it was then passed to the illuminator(s).

9a. The artist(s) are responsible for drawing and illuminating any initials, decoration and miniatures.

10. Under-drawing is conducted in hard-point, lead-point or ink, or sometimes in charcoal.

11. The process of illuminating begins with laying on gold (gilding), as this is the messiest stage.

12. A plaster-like substance (bole) is softened with beaten egg-white, applied to the area to be gilded and left to dry.

13. Gold leaf is laid down and sticks to the bole, aided by moisture from the illuminator's breath.

14. An agate or dogs-tooth is used to burnish the gold.

15. The body of the initial is painted with pigments, in this case a blue made from lapis lazuli mixed with beaten egg-white (glair).

16. The finished parchment leaves (folios) are now ready to be assembled into gatherings and bound as a book.

17. Binding usually consisted of sewing the quires successively onto leather cords (perhaps strung on a frame), the ends of which were then laced through holes in wooden boards and pegged into place with tiny wooden dowels. Further cords at the head and foot of

1

2

3

55–59. Making a medieval illuminated manuscript. Images from a 13th-cent. German manuscript, Copenhagen, Königliche Bibl., MS 4 2°, with the same processes being conducted by a modern calligrapher, Sally Teague, at the Roehampton Institute.

1. Parchmenter preparing parchment and showing it to the scribe.

2. Pricking and ruling the layout.

3. The scribe writes the text and then any rubrics (titles etc.) in red.

4. Recutting the quill's nib and erasing a whole sheet of text with pumice.

5. The illuminator paints any decoration, first laying down any gold, sometimes over a gesso ground, as seen on the right.

4

5

the spine, known as endbands, would also be sewn into place during sewing to consolidate the spine and prevent worming. The boards and spine were then covered with damp leather which was glued to the insides of the boards and perhaps covered with paste-downs (often fragments of earlier manuscripts). Straps or clasps would usually be added to keep the book in shape (as parchment tends to try to revert to the shape of the animal). The leather might be blind stamped or tooled or given gilded tooling, and met-alwork fittings or plaques (also sometimes of ivory) might be over-laid. Sometimes over-covers of fabric or sheepskin, known as chemises, were also used.

The people behind the words

We have already seen that in its early stages writing is often the preserve of an elite. In ancient Egypt only a tiny percentage of the population is thought to have been literate. This picture improved under the Greeks and changed radically under the Roman Empire. The archaeological record yields ample evidence of literacy at the level of the *plebs* (fig. 60), from graffiti on the walls of Pompeii to lead curse plaques beseeching the gods for revenge on irritating neighbours. Roman schoolrooms were well-ordered, following a syllabus of the liberal arts: the *trivium* (grammar, rhetoric and dialectic) and *quadrivium* (arithmetic, geometry, music and astronomy). Some of the wax tablets and papyrus scrolls on which Roman youngsters learned to write have survived. The slaves who underpinned society could also be highly literate, originating as they often did in centres of learning. Cicero's secretary, Tiro, was a freedman and invented one of the most popular tachygraphic (shorthand) systems of Antiquity – Tironian notes (fig. 61), which were still widely used in the early Middle Ages (the symbol for 'and', resembling an Arabic 7, can still be seen on some Irish road signs). It is important to remember that during Antiquity and much of the Middle Ages authors did not pen their own works, but dictated them to scribes, often using wax tablets as an interim drafting mechanism.

There were more 'public libraries' under Rome. Those founded by Augustus and of noblemen such as Sulla supplemented the provision of the great official libraries of Alexandria and Pergamum (which had been founded in the 3rd century BC and 196 BC respectively), and the temple repositories. Publishers, known from ancient Greece, also flourished and played a formative role in determining what has been transmitted to us. Cicero had trouble with his publisher who was in such a hurry to have his scribes prepare copies for distribution that Cicero was unable to make what he considered essential revisions at 'proof' stage, leading to

60. The baker Terentius Neo and his wife; a fresco from Pompeii, 1st cent. AD. Naples, Museo Archaeologico.

This fresco, buried in the eruption of Mount Vesuvius in AD 79, depicts Neo and his wife holding a papyrus scroll and wax tablets and stylus.

70

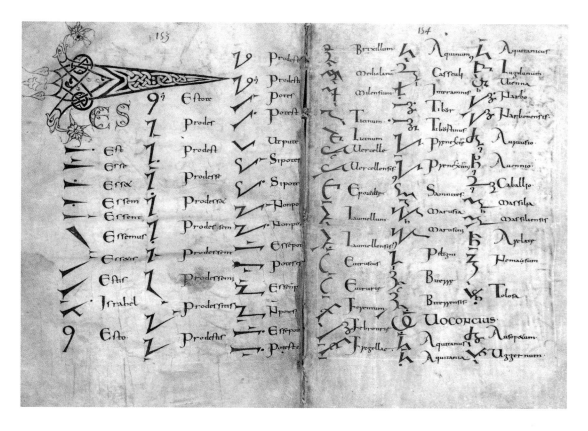

a first edition of some of his works which lacked authorial sanction (it still happens), the disgruntled author having to issue his own version through a different publishing house.

The early medieval world of Byzantium and the 'barbarian' successor states received the legacy of the professional scribe of Antiquity, whether literary or administrative, and of the educated person of the late Roman and early Christian world. This legacy had already undergone a process of selection of 'classics' in full or abbreviated 'Reader's Digest' form, and that of identifying canonical religious texts. In the eastern and southern Mediterranean much of the learning of Antiquity, including the works of Aristotle, passed under the guardianship of Islam, only to be regained by the West with the Crusades and the scholasticism of the 12th century.

In the early medieval world learning and literacy were primarily the preserves of the Church and book production the domain of the monastic scriptorium ('writing room'; *see* fig. 62). As such, reading

61. Shorthand symbols devised by Cicero's secretary, Tiro, in the first century BC, from a late 9th-cent. Carolingian lexicon This opening begins with signs for words containing the syllable 'es'.
BL, MSS, Add. MS 37518, ff. 77v–78.

71

and writing were open to a wide number of men and women of religious vocation and spread beyond the confines of the cloister through the education of the sons, and to a lesser extent daughters, of the nobility in church schools. Such educational provision varied; highpoints were often achieved in response to programmes of educational reform such as those instigated by the Emperor Charlemagne (who tried to become literate with only limited success late in life) in the late 8th to early 9th centuries and by Alfred the Great (himself a learned translator into Old English) at the end of the 9th century. The impression of clerical exclusivity should not be over-emphasised, for there is increasing evidence, albeit sparse, of lay involvement in literacy, such as that observed in the area of St Gall in Switzerland where lay scribes continued to produce charters. Laypeople also worked, possibly in collaboration, as artists. The Dover Bible, made at Christ Church Canterbury around 1150, depicts artists in lay dress in the act of painting its letters. Clerical scribes were also often extremely mobile; Eadui Basan

62. The medieval scriptorium. Carolingian ivory, 960–980. Kunsthistorisches Museum, Vienna.

St Gregory is shown writing, inspired by the Holy Spirit, whilst a group of clerics write below.

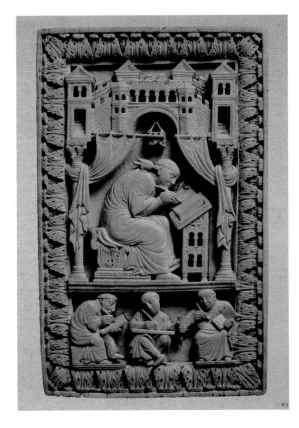

('Eadui the Fat'), for example, a Christ Church Canterbury monk of the early 11th century, was borrowed by King Cnut to write royal charters and worked on a number of *de luxe* manuscript commissions; he may have stimulated a colleague, Aelfric Bata, to lament the phenomenon of 'rock star' scribes who went on the road and earned money instead of staying at home teaching.

The working teams which operated in a church environment could vary greatly in composition. To take the example of the Lindisfarne scriptorium, a foundation of Celtic Columban origins in north-east England, around 700: library books could be the work of teams of as many as five or more scribes working in shifts, whereas what is probably its most magnificent and time-consuming work, the Lindisfarne Gospels (fig. 63), is the work of one master artist/scribe. Whoever this was had to fit the work (which modern calligraphers estimate at a minimum of two and a half years with the benefit of electric light and heating) around a monastic day entailing eight church services, personal prayer and study, domestic duties and possibly considerable administrative duties (if the 10th-century colophon is correct and the Gospels were the work of the bishop, Eadfrith). This is the work of a hero-scribe of the kind celebrated in contemporary poetry; an individual's *opus dei* ('work for God'). We are speaking of an environment in which sacred calligraphy, of a kind familiar to Islam, was a real consideration, when, as Cassiodorus said, every word written was a wound on Satan's body. In this context the effort lavished upon the intricate incipit (major text opening) pages in which the Word is made word becomes explicable as something beyond art for art's sake.

Generally artists and scribes were anonymous, but where colophons do occur only the scriptorium master or a flamboyant individual is usually named, concealing the identities of numerous collaborators. Such is the case with the Sherborne Missal of 1400–1407 in which images of the principal artist, the Dominican John Siferwas, and the scribe, the Benedictine John Whas, abound alongside those of their patrons, the Bishop of Salisbury and the Abbot of Sherborne, in what remains one of the greatest works of promotion and advertisement for sponsorship ever made (fig. 64).

The same is true of the secular workshops and ateliers which flourished during the high Middle Ages, such as that of the late 13th-century courtly Parisian artist Maître Honoré. With the rise of the universities around 1200, towns became the focus of book production, although clerics were still heavily involved either in church scriptoria or in the world at large if in non-claustral minor orders. The demands of students, which rapidly spilled over into the noble and mercantile classes, stimulated a thriving book trade staffed by men and women and manipulated by professional stationers (*librarii*,

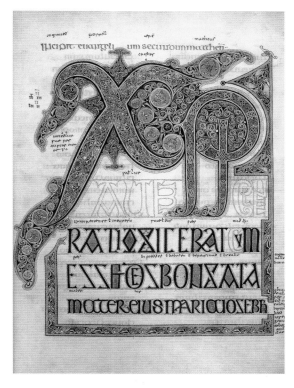

63. The Lindisfarne Gospels: incipit from St Matthew's Gospel commencing with the name of Christ in Greek characters, Lindisfarne, Northumbria, *c.* 698.
BL, MSS, Cotton MS Nero D.iv, f. 29.

Here the Word is made word. A supreme example of Christian sacred calligraphy in which the words themselves have almost become icons, at a time when every word written was considered a wound on Satan's body.

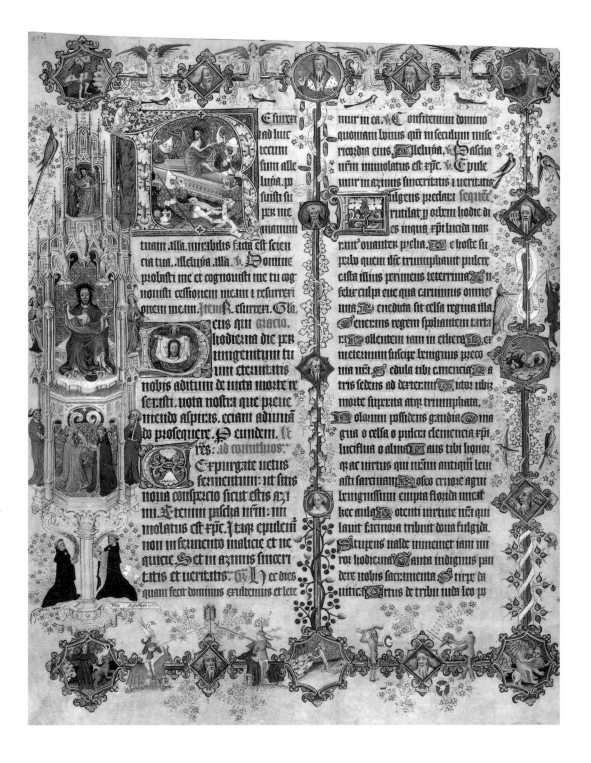

libraires, cartolai; see fig. 65) who operated a web of sub-contraction which embraced parchmenters, scribes and artists (who might specialise in miniatures or in other types of decoration such as pen-flourished borders). The stationers also sold materials which had traditionally been made at scriptorium centres (parchment, quills, styli, brushes, ink, pigments, etc.). They worked closely with patrons, each component of book manufacture being meticulously priced, be it grade of script or type of decorated initial. They also operated a system of 'piece work' with the university authorities, the *pecia* system, by which they rented out sections (*peciae*) of officially authorised texts to scribes and artists on a sub-contracting basis. This proliferation of specialisation and the de-centralisation of working teams led to an increase in the use of devices to enable work to be successfully assembled and bound: *pecia* marks themselves, quire numeration, quire signatures, catchwords (the first word of the next quire written at the end of a quire) and written instructions to artists and binders.

LEFT:

64. The Sherborne Missal: depiction of the patrons and craftsmen, *c.*1400–1407.
BL, MSS, Loan MS 82, p. 216.

The Dominican illuminator, John Siferwas, and the Benedictine scribe, John Whas, are depicted in the lower half of the left-hand border along with the Bishop of Salisbury and the Abbot of Sherborne, in one of the greatest statements of medieval patronage and sponsorship.

RIGHT:

65. Medieval stationers, 15th cent., Bologna.
Bologna, Biblioteca Universitaria, MS 963, f. 4.

The figure in the foreground is cutting parchment to size, whilst that in the rear is erasing text with pumice for reuse palimpsesting). Quills are hung for curing outside.

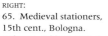

Sometimes books were bought 'off the peg' or were adapted for a buyer, perhaps by the addition of their arms or motto (as was the case with some of the books purchased by King Edward IV of England in the southern Netherlands), others were custom-made. An illuminated book of hours (a devotional aid which became one of the most popular books of the later Middle Ages) might cost a merchant a year's salary.

Occasionally authors themselves became personally involved in the publication of their works. One such was Matthew Paris, a 13th-century monk of St Albans who frequented court circles and who composed, edited, penned and illustrated his own historical works. Another was the early 15th-century French courtier Christine de Pisan (fig. 66) who, upon the deaths of her enlightened father and husband, decided to eschew remarriage or a life in the cloister in favour of earning a living for herself and her young children by her pen. From the heart-rending love poems through which she expressed her grief she moved to texts designed to enrich the life of the court, such as her *City of Women* and admonition to her son on how to survive in high circles. She seems to have acted as the scribe of her own works, by no means the norm with dictation still being generally favoured, and to have supervised and worked with a professional team of scribes and artists to produce fine copies of her works, fit for presentation to the Queen of France.

This practice of authorial participation was one heartily embraced by the Italian humanists, such as Petrarch, Collucio Salutati, Poggio Bracciolini and Niccolò Niccoli. They too chose to compose and edit texts, acting as their own scribes and, initially, distributors (fig. 67). This gave them the control necessary to launch the programme of cultural reform which spread out from early 15th-century Florence and other humanist centres such as Rome, Milan, Venice, Ferrara, Naples and Urbino, to form what we term the Renaissance. Their aims included

OPPOSITE:
66. Christine de Pisan: a medieval author/scribe at work, from her *Collected Works*, a copy which she 'published' herself for presentation to the Queen of France.
BL, MSS, Harley MS 4431, f. 4.

67. Origins of the Italian humanist manuscript: an essay in desk-top publishing. This section of a copy of Livy's *History* was written by the hand of one of the key instigators of humanism, Petrarch, in Avignon, 1325–9.
BL, MSS, Harley MS 2493, f. 92.

emancipation from an essentially theocratic culture and one moulded by Imperial Germanic/ Gothic domination. As a visible sign of this the humanists espoused reforms of script, decoration and codicology (the way in which books are physically structured). For their script they chose as a base Caroline minuscule (ironically popularised by Charlemagne's imperial programme of cultural reform) modelled upon that found in northern Italian manuscripts of the 12th century. These were also the source of the characteristic white-vine ornament which abounds alongside classical vases, cartouches and putti (cherubs). The scripts of the humanists formed the basis of the early typefaces, roman and italic, although in northern Europe Gothic script informed early German type fonts.

The possibilities of desk-top publishing incorporating the sophisticated interaction of text and image, as espoused by authors such as Matthew Paris, Christine de Pisan and the humanists, have only recently become available to us again through our electronic media, which can now, theoretically if not in practice, be exploited by a broad sector of the world's population.

The evolution of western scripts

How then was the development of western handwriting (*see* fig. 68) moulded by considerations of form and function, technology and history?

The Roman system of scripts, prevalent from the 1st century BC to around AD 600 and the pontificate of the missionising Pope Gregory the Great, encompassed a hierarchy in which function was paramount and technology influenced form. The earliest, most formal script was 'Square Capitals' whose angular forms were ideally suited to production by the chisel but ill-suited to the pen which produced a more fluid variety know as 'Rustic Capitals' (*see* figs. 68–69). Ironically, no sooner did the stonemasons observe this than they translated these liquid forms back into the equally unsuitable medium of stone (carved rustics are known as *scriptura actuaria*). When written cursively, as graffiti or on wax tablets, capitals became diffuse in form with fewer strokes, often subtly changing their appearance as some elements became more discreet or disappeared (such as the cross-stroke of 'A'). This script was widely used for secretarial purposes and is known as 'Old Roman Cursive'. From the 2nd to the 4th centuries

1. Egyptian hieroglyphs.   3,100 BC–AD 300

2. Phoenician.   1200–200 BC

3. Greek.   1000 BC–the present

4–6. Old Roman system.   30 BC–AD 300
4. Roman Square Capitals.

5. Roman Rustic Capitals.

6. Old Roman cursive.

7–9. New Roman system.   AD 300– 600
(300–850 for 9)
7. Uncial.

8. New Roman Cursive

9. Half-uncial.

10. Merovingian Chancery Script.   AD 600–800

11. Caroline Minuscule.   AD 800–1250

12. Gothic Book Script (textualis)   AD 1200–1600

13. English Cursive.   AD 1175–1650

14. French Cursive (secretary).   AD 1300–1650

15. Bastard Secretary.   AD 1400–1650

16. Humanistic Cursive.   AD 1400–1700

17. Humanistic Book Script.   AD 1400–1700

18. Roman Typeface.   1475– the present

68. The evolution of letter-forms in the West, from Egyptian hiero-glyphs to Renaissance typefaces (artwork by Patricia Lovett after Michelle Brown).

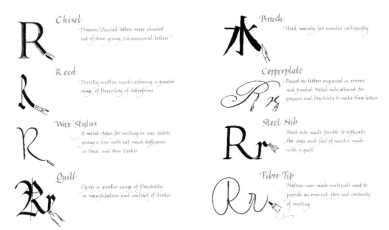

How Writing Tools have influenced Letterforms

Chisel
Drawn / Painted letters were chiselled out of stone, giving 3 dimensional letters

Reed
Directly written marks allowing a greater range of flexibility of letterforms

Wax Stylus
A metal stylus for writing on wax tablets giving a line with not much difference in thick and thin strokes

Quill
Gives a greater range of flexibility in manipulation and contrast of strokes

Brush
Used mainly for oriental calligraphy

Copperplate
Based on letters engraved in reverse and printed. Metal nibs allowed for pressure and flexibility to make these letters

Steel Nib
Steel nibs made possible to replicate the style and feel of marks made with a quill

Fibre Tip
Modern man made materials used to provide an even ink flow and continuity of writing

69. The influence of writing implements upon scripts (artwork by Satwinder Sehmi).

AD the New Roman system emerged, with capitals developing into more rounded 'Uncial' forms with the use of the pen and under some cursive influence. These scripts were written with a slanted pen in which the nib is cut at a right angle to the shaft and which, given the natural slant of the arm and pen during writing, produces a slanted top to minims (the upright strokes of letters). The use of a straight pen in which the nib is cut at an angle to compensate for the slant during writing, producing straight tops to minims, led to a more upright ductus and a tendency to produce extended upright backs and tails to letters such as 'd' and 'q' (rather than 'D' and 'Q') in a script known as 'Half-Uncial' which became the main book script (along with uncials for very luxurious works). The tendency in half-uncial to introduce 'lower case' letter forms was increased by the influence of 'New Roman Cursive', the result of bureaucratic reforms of the early 4th century, which increased speed by the introduction of loops to letters such as 'd' and 'l' and by joining letters up (sometimes by means of ligatures in which a stroke of one letter also forms part of the next). A mixture of the two scripts produced 'Cursive Half-Uncial', the hand of the educated person of late Antiquity.

This was the legacy of Antiquity to the post-Roman world – one which was to keep re-emerging at certain historical points as part of the quest to regain that Antique past which we term 'renaissance'. On the Continent the Franks and the Byzantines, through their Italian outpost of Ravenna, perpetuated the secretarial script New Roman Cursive, its impulse towards overly cursive illegibility reaching new heights and approaching what has been described as the 'wanderings of a demented spider' in Merovingian chancery cursive. For high-grade books the Franks and Christian Rome used uncials. In answer to the need for a middle grade between these two extremes of formality various centres experimented with fusions of their own, often pro-ducing 'minuscule' scripts (lower case scripts which, with their ascending and descending strokes to 'd', 'q' etc., occupy four lines, like cursive, rather than the two lines of 'majuscule' scripts such as uncial) – for example, Luxeuil minuscule and Corbie 'ab' minuscule. The south of Italy produced its own local variant in the mid-8th century, Beneventan minuscule, which survived until 1300 (and until the 15th century in conservative centres) and the Visigoths produced Visig-othic minuscule which survived until the reconquests of Spain from Islam in the 12th century. A process of vulgarisation of script may be observed, akin to that experienced linguistically in the development of the romance languages from their Latin base.

The Insular world (Britain and Ireland), some of which had not experienced intensive Roman rule, escaped the legacy of secretarial cursive and reinvented its own hierarchical system of scripts, taking as its starting point cursive half-uncial, the hand of the early missionar-ies of the post-Romano-British Church, such as Sts Patrick and Ninian. Under growing Roman influence, in the wake of St Augus-tine's mission to Kent in 597, this system grew to include display cap-itals based upon square, rustic, uncial and indigenous letter-forms (possibly influenced by runes), uncial, a beautifully calligraphic Insu-lar version of half-uncial, and a range of cursives of varying degrees of formality. Gospel books and high-grade liturgical manuscripts employed the formal, time-consuming uncials and half-uncials, whilst library books and those published for wide circulation and export (such as Bede's *History of the English Church and People*) were written in elegant legible cursives. Most documents were also cursive although some of the earliest are written in the higher grade uncials, betraying a perception of the elevated status of writing moulded by its use in a Christian liturgical context. This perception ultimately led Archbishop Wulfred in the early 9th century to make the first presen-tation of written evidence at law, thereby asserting the primacy of writing over centuries of oral witness. Other important developments included the Irish introduction of word separation (Antiquity employing a *scriptura continua* without breaks) and greater use of punctuation through a system of points (*distinctiones*), the rising number of which indicated a rising value of pause (one = comma, two = colon, three = full stop), in a manner reminiscent of the arrangement of ogham characters denoted by a rising number of lines. An interest in such devices sprang from the process of acquiring literacy and of learning Latin as a foreign language, along with a growing trend towards silent meditative reading and comprehension rather than the oral delivery which was taught by Roman schools where actors were often employed to instruct students in how to articulate written texts as oration. No sooner were these lessons learnt than they were applied to the vernacular, making Old Irish and Old English the most precocious written European vernaculars. Insular artists and scribes also made a definitive contribution to book production by the way in which they used ornament, often as part of script itself, to articulate the text, marking key text breaks with decorated initials and integrating text and image through the introduction of devices such as historiated (story-telling) initials and complex symbolic images which are meant to be 'read'. The illuminated manuscript never looked back.

During the 9th century the Insular achievement was temporarily eclipsed by Viking raids and settlement. This century also witnessed the diffusion of one of the most influential of scripts – 'Caroline minuscule'. This was developed in centres such as Corbie and Tours from an essentially uncial/half-uncial/local minuscule base as an adjunct to the dissemination of authorised texts as part of the religious and cultural reforms instigated by the Emperor Charlemagne and his English advisor, Alcuin of York, from the end of the 8th century onwards. It was thus the result of an officially sponsored publication programme and, through Carolingian conquests and political influence, spread throughout much of Europe, supplanting the national hands except in areas which escaped subjugation, notably Beneventan Italy, much of Visigothic/Mozarabic Spain, the Celtic West (Ireland continuing to practise an Insular cursive into this century) and, initially, Anglo-Saxon England. England is an interesting case. Following the offensives against the Vikings and the educational and religious reforms of Alfred the Great in the late 9th century, it used an Anglo-Saxon minuscule (the aspect of which varied over time from pointed to square to rounded) until, under increasing Carolingian cultural influence, Caroline minuscule was introduced in the second half of the 10th century. Even then the English were reluctant to relinquish their own scriptual identity and used Caroline for texts in Latin and their own minuscule for Old English, often side by side in bilingual translations – the ultimate English solution to 'Europeanism'.

On the Continent Caroline was used for nearly everything (although some other more cursive, stylised scripts were used for document production in the imperial and Roman chanceries). It was clear, comparatively easy to write, and accompanied by devices such as a more developed punctuation system, using diacritical signs, and neumes for musical notation (punctuation was subsequently further developed by the scholastics and the humanists). It was initially written as a small rounded script, but over time its appearance changed significantly as it adopted an attenuated oval aspect during the Romanesque period (later 11th to 12th centuries), termed 'Protogothic script', and a fussy, compressed square aspect during the Gothic period (around 1200 – 1500) for formal Gothic book script (Gothic *textualis/textura*/black letter). It is the aspect and the details of script which make these forms look so very different; the letters remain essentially Caroline. English scribes liked to added calligraphic details to their treatment of Caroline, adding feet to minims (upright strokes) in the form of wedges or serifs. The political ascendancy of the Normans and Angevins and the rise of an international urban network of production led to the spread of such features, resulting in a virtually pan-European formal Gothic script (divided into grades of formality according to the detail and amount of effort required in production, which carried a price tag, and supplemented by smaller versions for glossing and annotation). The Angevin chancery in England was also responsible for the development of an impressive cursive script, suited to its high output, which reintroduced a fully cursive, thin script with loops to Europe in the late 12th century. By the late 13th century, with the widespread reintroduction of the thin pointed quill pen, this English cursive (*cursiva anglicana*) was being used for lower-grade books and was suited to the rigours of the urbanised book trade and to administrative purposes, being joined in the early 14th century by the prickly French 'secretary' script. The formal Gothic book script (*textualis*) remained in use for liturgical and other high-class books, but during the 14th century a plethora of compromise scripts emerged

70. Copperplate script, along with specimens (opposite) of late medieval and 'modern' hands, from one of the greatest of the writing masters' books, George Bickham's *Universal Penman* (London 1733–41).

ALPHABETS

In all the Hands now Practis'd in Great-Britain,

With Sentences in Prose and Verse, &c.

Written, and Engrav'd by.

George Bickham, Senior.

ROUND HAND.

Aaabbcddesffghhijkkllmnop
pqr.sfsttujvnxyyzz.&
ABCDEFGHIJKLM
NOPQRSTUVWXYZ.

Education either makes or
marrs us; and Governments, as
well as private Families, are con-
cerned in the Consequences of it.

RUNNING HAND.

Aaabbccddesffghijklmnopqrsstuvwxyyzz.
ABCDEFGHIJKKLLMMN
NOPQRSTUVWXXYYZ.

Virtue and Arts are attained by frequent Practice.

Know, all the Good that Individuals find,
Or God and Nature meant to meer Mankind,
Reason's whole Pleasures, all the Joys of Sense,
Lie in three Words, Health, Peace, and Competence.

ITALIAN.

Aaabbccddesffghijklmnopqrsstuvwxyyz;
ABCDEFGHIJKLLMMN
NOOPQRSTUVWWXXYYZ.

Bad Examples are of dangerous Consequence.

Riches and Plenty are the natural Fruits of
Liberty, and where these abound, Learning
and all the Liberal Arts will immediately
Lift up their Heads, Thrive, and Flourish.

1234567890.

SQUARE TEXT.

Aabcdefffghijkkllmm
nopqrxrstuvwxyyz.
ABCDEFGHIJKLM
NOPQRSTVWXYZ.

GERMAN TEXT.

Aabcdefghijkllmmnoop
pqqrrsstuvwxyyzz.
ABCDEFGHIJKLM
NOPQRSTUWXYZ.

INGROSSING.

Aaabbudeeefffghijkllm
nopqrrfsottuvvwxyyzz.
ABCDEFGHIJKLM
NOPQRSTVWXYZ.

INGROSSING.

The Pen an Instrument tho' small,
Is of great Use and Benefit to all.
Trust rather to your fingers Ends,
Than to the Promises of friends.

GERMAN TEXT.

Speaking is vocal Thought;
Thinking is silent Speach;
but Writing is the Image
or Character of them Both.

SECRETARY.

Aaabbccddeesffghijklmnopqrsstuvwxyz.
ABCDEFGGHIJKLLMN
OPPQRSTUVWXYZZ.

Despise not but pity human Infirmities.

OLD ENGLISH PRINT.

A aabcdefghijklmnopqrsstu
vwxxyyzz.
ABCDEFGHIKLMN
OPQRSTUWXXYZ.

Of Art, so just a Share to each is sent,
That the most Avaritious are content.
For none e'er thought, y due Division's such,
His own too little, or his Friend's too much.

ROMAN PRINT.

Aabcdefghijklmnopqrstuvwxyz.
ABCDEFGHIJKLMNO
PQRSTUVWXYZ.

Good Understanding gaineth Favour.

No Art without a Genius will prevail,
And Parts without y help of Art will fail;
But both Ingredients jointly must unite,
To make the happy Character compleat.

1234567890.

ITALICK PRINT.

Aabcdefghijkl mnopqrstuvwxyz.
ABCDEFGHIJKLMNOP
PQRSTUVWXYZ.

Prodigality is ever attended by Injustice and Folly.

Much in the Knife may lie, much in the Quill,
But infinitely more resides in Skill.
The Knife 'tis cuts the Pen, the Pen the Letter,
But he that Wants the Art is ne'er the better.

VIVE LA PLUME.

To Willm Caslon Esqr one of His Majesties Justices of the Peace for the County of Middlesex. This Plate is most humbly Dedicated by George Bickham, Senior.

LONDON: Sold by Geo Bickham in Featherstone-Street, Bunhill-Fields.

71. Calligraphy by Edward
Johnston, 1908.
BL, MSS, Add. MS 54250, f.1.

Johnston, 'The Father of
modern calligraphy', devised
a foundational hand, to
reform modern handwriting
and based it upon a late
10th-cent. Anglo-Saxon
Caroline minuscule hand in
BL, Harley MS 2904.

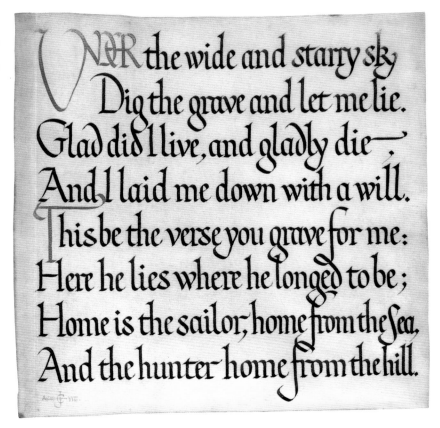

Under the wide and starry sky
Dig the grave and let me lie.
Glad did I live, and gladly die,
And I laid me down with a will.
This be the verse you grave for me:
Here he lies where he longed to be;
Home is the sailor, home from the sea,
And the hunter home from the hill.

from an admix of formal and cursive features (termed 'bastard' or 'hybrid', as in 'Bastard anglicana', 'Bastard secretary' and 'hybrida', along with an artificially produced *textualis* termed 'fere-textualis/ fere-textura'). During the 15th and 16th centuries even the most luxurious of romances and histories penned for the Burgundian, French and English courts would employ a stylish formally written Bastard secretary script – Bâtarde.

In Italy the influence of Caroline was more overt throughout the Middle Ages, Italian Gothic *textualis rotunda* being more rounded and less prone to lateral compression and elaboration (only the university town of Bologna favouring some compression along northern European lines). Nonetheless, the intelligentsia of late 14th-century Florence who gave birth to the humanist movement which underpinned the Renaissance reacted against what they perceived as Gothic/Imperial domination. Their reforms in book production, fuelled by their own roles as authors/scribes, led them to revise the script, ornament and codicological practices of an earlier age, ironically focusing on the imperially inspired Caroline minuscule, as found in northern Italian manuscripts of the 12th century. Their formal script (*lettera antica*) and their cursive (including the calligraphic variety, *cancellaresca*, developed by Ludovico degli Arrighi, a scribe of the Apostolic Chancery and author of the first printed writing book, *La Operina*, Rome, 1522) formed the basis of the 15th-century Italian typefaces, roman and italic, which are with us still.

The advent of printing did not end handwriting, as we have seen. Bob Cratchett and his fellow scriveners underpinned administrative and commercial record-keeping until supplanted by the typist, stenographer and VDU operator. All literate souls needed to write and since the time of Arrighi generations of writing masters (including Edward Cocker, George Bickham and John Jenkins) tried to instil good practice amongst learners through their printed copybooks, the thin, curvaceous script known as 'Copperplate' representing their response to the need to engrave scripts on metal plates for reproduction (fig. 70). This is known in the USA as 'Spencerian' after Platt Rogers Spencer (1800–1864) who promoted it for business use. Teaching methods such as the cumbersome 'push-pull' exercises of the Palmer Method abounded. Calligraphers have preserved the art of fine writing and in the 20th century their impact was more widely felt through the reforms of Edward Johnston who, in humanist fashion, looked to a late 10th-century Anglo-Saxon manuscript written in English Caroline minuscule, the Ramsey Psalter (BL, Harley MS 2904), as the inspiration for his 'foundational hand' (*see* fig. 71). This is still taught to aspiring modern calligraphers and, like Alfred Fairbank's revival of italic, has exerted a beneficial (if still all too limited) effect upon modern western handwriting.

FOUR

Where is writing going?

We have seen that handwriting has withstood and responded to a wide range of technological challenges over the centuries. Along with the principal vehicle of writing in the West – the book – it has witnessed the introduction of print, recorded sound and film and now the electronic medium. But does it have a future?

For some time there has been a debate in educationalist circles concerning whether people now need to be taught how to write at all, or whether we should concentrate on keyboarding skills. This issue has recently been overtaken by the advent of voice-activated computers which convert the sounds of a human voice into electronic impulses to produce writing on the screen. Your immediate reaction to this may be to to unplug your laptop and reach for a paper and pen, or to banish such outmoded devices as handwriting from your life forever. But let us consider the underlying principles of information transmission and see if there is in fact any precedent for such a scenario. The closest one is probably that of Graeco-Roman Antiquity in which an author would not write his works down, but would compose and deliver them orally (*see* fig. 72). As the orator spoke, a scribe would often commit their words to writing, usually on wax tablets for working-up subsequently as fair copies, undoubtedly making errors in translating what he heard into written form (similar problems of voice recognition are now being encountered in electronic form). Is this so very different to voice activation, but with the scribe and his tablets fulfilling the role of the computer? The technology may bear comparison, but what *is* different is that the classical author was rigorously

72. A classical orator whose words are recorded by a scribe on wax tablets. Christ before Pilate, from the Rossano Gospels, Syria, 6th cent. Rossano (Calabria), Il Duomo di Rossano, Rossano Gospels, f. 8v.

taught to compose and convey his texts mentally and orally – we are not. Our memories are not trained in this way; we need to interact with the graphic image of our own words if we are to produce any but the shortest or most basic forms of information. We still need hard-copy and, dare one say it, the book to appreciate the entirety of our creation.

This does not, of course, mean of itself that we need handwriting, but a survey of the evolution of writing has shown us that some societies and writing systems definitely still do, unless they are irrevocably to relinquish their traditions to the dictates of the computer. The social inequalities of access to electronic technology are also beginning to be perceived as a problem. We have also seen that writing and its technology has generally operated by adapting form to need. We need not take the over-simplistic either/or option but may enjoy the best of all worlds, suiting form to function and revelling in a pluralistic information system and technology.

The way in which information has been conveyed in the past has a lot to offer in helping us to explore our own rapidly developing Information Technology and its applications. Good design principles for letter-forms and fonts, reading issues such as combating eye-skip, and the inter-relationship of text and image are all areas which have been addressed in earlier times and from which we may learn. The 13th to

73. The eroticism of writing. Still from Peter Greenaway's film *The Pillow Book*.

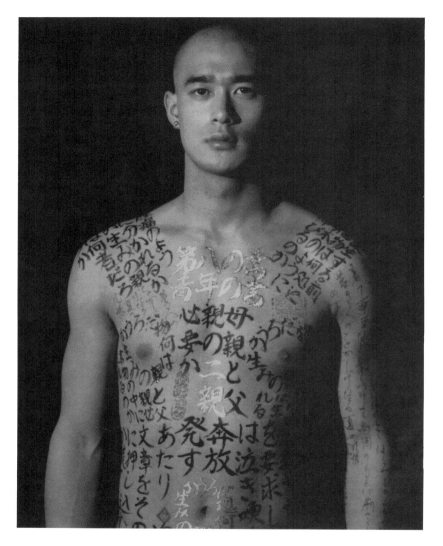

14th-century western biblical and legal texts with their numerous layers of wrap-round glosses and commentaries, and the parallel columns of multi-lingual translations with their cross-referencing apparatus, have much to teach us about intertextuality. Likewise, the rubrics of complex liturgical volumes display an awareness of the concept of 'hyper-text', whilst the 9th-century audience of the influential Carolingian Utrecht Psalter was well able to mentally 'click on' a detail of its images, relate it to a passage of text and provide a raft of underlying exegetical interpretation, foreshadowing electronic applications

90

of intertextuality. An appreciation of the grades of script mastered by professional scribes and of the hierarchical structure of form and function should also allow us to consider which are the most appropriate modes of communication for different types of information and contexts. Our automated and handwritten instruments of writing have different presentation needs and our handwriting, when we use it, should not be so ill-disciplined that it always deteriorates into a cursive script, illegible sometimes even to our own eyes. Time spent practising writing, experimenting with degrees of formality, speed and different writing implements, is a good investment in self-image and allows us to tap into millennia of human development. The physical

74. 'War' by Satwinder Sehmi, 1996, an example of modern calligraphy as fine art.

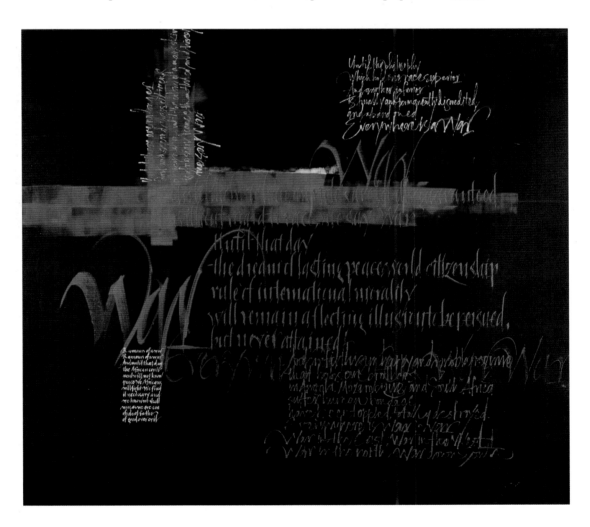

act of writing also plays an essential role in the process of learning to read and to memorise words.

In this increasingly energy-conscious, if not responsible, age it would be foolhardy to relinquish manual writing skills which, even alongside invaluable mechanical and electronic aids, continue to fulfil a useful role in their immediacy and inherent portability. As an art form calligraphy, perpetually valued in oriental, Indian and Islamic contexts, is undergoing a western renaissance of its own, producing works of fine art such as Donald Jackson's 'Painting with Words' series and the work of many other fine contemporary calligraphers (*see* fig. 74). At street level the graffiti 'taggers' (whose work is simultaneously celebrated and denigrated by commentators such as Iain Sinclair) find it as effective a mode of communication as did their Roman counterparts in Pompeii on the eve of Mount Vesuvius' eruption. The erotic nature of reading and writing and their psychological benefits should not be ignored either. One does not readily curl up before the fire, under an apple tree or in a bath with a laptop and Peter Greenaway's film, *The Pillow Book* (*see* fig. 73), would have belonged to a very different genre, more appropriate to Quentin Tarantino, had it involved the transmission of electronic impulses to the human skin and nerve-endings rather than the sensuous strokes of the calligrapher.

Our handwriting says at least as much about us as the way we dress (unfortunately we do not often invest as much in it) and can provide a vantage point to our inner selves, as graphologists and management consultants would be the first to confirm. Its value and totemic significance is recognised in those very places which might be expected to eschew it – the corridors of high-tech mercantile power. To quote Edward Tenner on technology and the 'revenge effect' in *Why Things Bite Back*, 'Modern presentations, like the Victorians' efforts, have a scale of values. The problem is that as elegant laser output gets more affordable and 'mail-merge' programs make customised form letters almost effortless, handwriting has moved up to the top of the executive communication scale. Top-of-the-line Montblanc, Waterman, Parker and Pelikan fountain pens cost more than many computer printers. The head of Montblanc's US operations believes that when word processing removed the prestige once enjoyed by a flawless letter that only a top executive secretary could have typed, the handwritten note took its place.'

One way or another, writing is here to stay.

Further reading

General: history of writing

David Diringer, *A History of the Alphabet* (London 1953; 3rd edn Henley-on-Thames, 1983)

H. Jensen, *Sign, Symbol and Script* (London & New York, 1969)

Donald Jackson, *The Story of Writing* (London, 1981)

Albertine Gaur, *A History of Writing* (London, 1984; 3rd edn 1992)

Roy Harris, *The Origin of Writing* (London, 1986)

J. David Bolter, *Writing Space: the Computer, Hypertext and the History of Writing* (1991)

Karen Brookfield, *Writing*, Dorling Kindersley Eyewitness Guides (London, 1993), for children and as a picture source

Albertine Gaur, *A History of Calligraphy* (London, 1994)

Andrew Robinson, *The Story of Writing* (London, 1995)

Roy Harris, *Signs, Language and Communication, Integrational and Segregational Approaches* (London, 1996)

P. T. Daniels and W. Bright, eds, *The World's Writing Systems* (Oxford, 1996)

The Medieval West: book production, palaeography and codicology

M. T. Clanchy, *From Memory to Written Record* (London & Cambridge, 1979)

B. Stock, *The Implications of Literacy, Written Language and Models of Interpretation in the 11th and 12th Centuries* (Princeton, 1983)

Elmar Mittler, ed., *Skriptorium. Die Buchherstellung im Mittelalter von Vera Trost* (catalogue of 'Biblioteca Palatina' exhibition, University of Heidelberg, 1986)

Jean Glenisson, ed., *Le Livre au Moyen Age* (Paris, 1988)

Leonard Boyle, *Medieval Latin Palaeography: a Bibliographical Introduction* (Toronto, 1984)

O. Weijers, ed., *Vocabulaire du Livre et de l'Ecriture au Moyen Age* (Turnhout, 1989)

Jacques Lemaire, *Introduction à la Codicologie* (Louvain-la-Neuve, 1989)

Bernard Bischoff, *Latin Palaeography* (Cambridge, 1990)

R. McKitterick, ed., *The Uses of Literacy in Early Medieval Europe* (Cambridge, 1990)

Michelle P. Brown, *A Guide to Western Historical Scripts from Antiquity to 1600* (London & Toronto, 1990; 2nd edn 1993)

R. Dale and R. Weaver, *Machines in the Office* (London, 1993)

The Illuminated Manuscript

D. V. Thompson, *Materials and Techniques of Medieval Painting* (New York, 1956)

Christopher de Hamel, *A History of Illuminated Manuscripts* (Oxford, 1986)

Christopher de Hamel, *Scribes and Illuminators* (London, 1992)

Jonathan J. G. Alexander, *Medieval Illuminators and Their Methods of Work* (London & New Haven, 1992)

Michelle P. Brown, *Understanding Illuminated Manuscripts, a Guide to Technical Terms* (London & Malibu, 1994)

J. M. Backhouse, *The Illuminated Page* (London, 1997)

Index

March 22/07